BEST-LOVED
POEMS

BEST-LOVED POEMS

POEMS

A Treasury
of Verse

Michael O'Mara Books Limited

First published in Great Britain in 2017
by Michael O'Mara Books Limited

9 Lion Yard
Tremadoc Road
London SW4 7NQ

Papers used by Michael O'Mara Books Limited are natural,
recyclable products made from wood grown in sustainable forests.
The manufacturing processes conform to the environmental
regulations of the country of origin.

ISBN: 978-1-78243-724-6 in hardback print format

1 2 3 4 5 6 7 8 9 10

www.mombooks.com

Designed and typeset by Ed Pickford

Cover design by Anna Morrison

Printed and bound by CPI Group (UK) Ltd, Croydon, CR0 4YY

For Laura, who will start telling me off for
skipping verses soon enough.

CONTENTS

INTRODUCTION

Poetry is personal. The poet tells us about love, grief, faith, doubt, fear or courage as they have felt it, and a receptive reader – sometimes centuries later – discovers that the verses strike a chord, and that scraps of the poem catch in their memory for ever. Any anthology of best-loved poems must, therefore, open with a sincere apology for omissions. Our unique private canon will be influenced by our age, our friends and families, our schooling and all our triumphs and tribulations, so it would be impossible to include everyone's favourites within these covers. Some longer poems have been cut due to limited space, but I hope the lines included give a flavour of the whole work and will inspire readers to seek out and savour the full texts.

We soak up poetry from our very earliest days. My three-year-old daughter already has a mental storehouse replete with nursery verses and rhyming stories, and as a result is acquainted with a host of characters from Bo Peep, through the Owl and the Pussy-Cat, to the Gruffalo. (Woe betide me if I attempt to skip a few lines in order to hasten bedtime – she is word perfect.) At the other end of life, people often retain fragments of favourite poems even when other memories become elusive. Poetry is successfully used as a therapeutic tool to unlock emotions and recollections in patients with dementia. Since we carry our favourite verses all our lives, I hope that any unfamiliar works included here will become new treasures to be enjoyed and stored.

This anthology is divided thematically so that readers can find a poem to suit any mood, though there is of course some fluidity in the categories. One of the beauties of poetry is its ability to address – often in just a handful of words – numerous big questions and passions at once. Blake and Hopkins find God in the contemplation of birds and beasts, for example, and Shelley sees his desire for his lover reflected in every corner of the natural world.

As readers we take comfort in knowing we are not alone in our struggles, and thrill to find words that express – more clearly and beautifully than we ever could – our joys. In a frenetic digital world it is a pure and restorative pleasure to sit for a few minutes with a poem, to chew and swallow its syllables slowly by reading it aloud, giving ourselves time to digest its language and rhythm as well as its truth. Poetry can connect us to others and to our own emotions in a profound and valuable way that we need now more than ever in a hyper-connected world that can feel superficial. It has been a privilege and indulgence to spend time seeking out these poems, and I hope you will enjoy reading them as much as I have.

COME LIVE WITH ME:
FANTASIES AND INFATUATIONS

We must begin with love, since any collection of treasured poems is bound to be saturated with all the infinite varieties of its pleasure and pain. This opening selection deals with the first flush of dizzy desire. The beloved is glimpsed but not yet grasped; the object of the poet's fevered fantasy is still just that, though Herrick and Marvell pant persuasively for consummation in these elegant verses of seduction. We must be grateful that the poor poets were so often lovelorn, since their yearning words speak eloquently to every age in which one person sighs for another.

She Walks in Beauty

GEORGE GORDON, LORD BYRON

She walks in beauty, like the night
    Of cloudless climes and starry skies;
And all that's best of dark and bright
    Meet in her aspect and her eyes:
Thus mellow'd to that tender light
    Which heaven to gaudy day denies.

One shade the more, one ray the less,
    Had half impair'd the nameless grace
Which waves in every raven tress,
    Or softly lightens o'er her face;
Where thoughts serenely sweet express
    How pure, how dear their dwelling place.

And on that cheek, and o'er that brow,
    So soft, so calm, yet eloquent,
The smiles that win, the tints that glow,
    But tell of days in goodness spent,
A mind at peace with all below,
    A heart whose love is innocent!

The Passionate Shepherd to His Love

CHRISTOPHER MARLOWE

Come live with mee, and be my love,
And we will all the pleasures prove,
That Vallies, groves, hills and fieldes,
Woods or steepie mountaine yeeldes.

And wee will sit upon the Rocks,
Seeing the Sheepheards feede theyr flocks,
By shallow Rivers, to whose falls,
Melodious byrds sing Madrigalls.

And I will make thee beds of Roses,
And a thousand fragrant posies,
A cap of flowers, and a kirtle,
Imbroydred all with leaves of Mirtle.

A gowne made of the finest wooll,
Which from our pretty Lambes we pull,
Fayre linèd slippers for the cold:
With buckles of the purest gold.

A belt of straw, and Ivie buds,
With Corall clasps and Amber studs,
And if these pleasures may thee move,
Come live with mee, and be my love.

The Sheepheards Swaines shall daunce and sing,
For thy delight each May-morning.
If these delights thy minde may move;
Then live with mee, and be my love.

First Love

JOHN CLARE

I ne'er was struck before that hour
    With love so sudden and so sweet,
Her face it bloomed like a sweet flower
    And stole my heart away complete.
My face turned pale as deadly pale.
    My legs refused to walk away,
And when she looked, what could I ail?
    My life and all seemed turned to clay.

And then my blood rushed to my face
    And took my eyesight quite away,
The trees and bushes round the place
    Seemed midnight at noonday.
I could not see a single thing,
    Words from my eyes did start –
They spoke as chords do from the string,
    And blood burnt round my heart.

Are flowers the winter's choice?
    Is love's bed always snow?
She seemed to hear my silent voice,
    Not love's appeals to know.
I never saw so sweet a face
    As that I stood before.
My heart has left its dwelling-place
    And can return no more.

Song

To Celia

BEN JONSON

Drinke to me, onely, with thine eyes,
 And I will pledge with mine;
Or leave a kisse but in the cup,
 And Ile not looke for wine.
The thirst, that from the soule doth rise,
 Doth aske a drinke divine:
But might I of JOVE's *Nectar* sup,
 I would not change for thine.

I sent thee, late, a rosy wreath,
 Not so much honoring thee,
As giving it a hope, that there
 It could not withered bee.
But thou thereon did'st onely breathe,
 And sent'st it backe to mee:
Since when it growes, and smells, I sweare,
 Not of it selfe, but thee.

[after the Greek of Philostratus]

Love's Philosophy

PERCY BYSSHE SHELLEY

The fountains mingle with the river,
    And the rivers with the ocean;
The winds of heaven mix forever,
    With a sweet emotion;
Nothing in the world is single;
    All things by a law divine
In one another's being mingle:
    Why not I with thine?

See! the mountains kiss high heaven,
    And the waves clasp one another;
No sister flower would be forgiven
    If it disdained its brother;
And the sunlight clasps the earth,
    And the moonbeams kiss the sea:
What are all these kissings worth,
    If thou kiss not me?

I Wanna Be Yours

JOHN COOPER CLARKE

I wanna be your vacuum cleaner
Breathing in your dust
I wanna be your Ford Cortina
I will never rust
If you like your coffee hot
Let me be your coffee pot
You call the shots
I wanna be yours

I wanna be your raincoat
For those frequent rainy days
I wanna be your dreamboat
When you want to sail away
Let me be your teddy bear
Take me with you anywhere
I don't care
I wanna be yours

I wanna be your electric meter
I will not run out
I wanna be the electric heater
You'll get cold without
I wanna be your setting lotion
Hold your hair in deep devotion
Deep as the deep Atlantic ocean
That's how deep is my devotion

To His Coy Mistress

ANDREW MARVELL

Had we but World enough, and Time,
This coyness Lady were no crime.
We would sit down, and think which way
To walk, and pass our long Loves Day.
Thou by the *Indian Ganges* side
Should'st Rubies find: I by the Tide
Of *Humber* would complain. I would
Love you ten years before the Flood:
And you should if you please refuse
Till the Conversion of the *Jews*.
My vegetable Love should grow
Vaster than Empires, and more slow.
An hundred years should go to praise
Thine Eyes, and on thy Forehead Gaze.
Two hundred to adore each Breast:
But thirty thousand to the rest.
An Age at least to every part,
And the last Age should show your Heart.
For Lady you deserve this State;
Nor would I love at lower rate.

But at my back I alwaies hear
Times wingèd Charriot hurrying near:

And yonder all before us lye
Desarts of vast Eternity.
Thy Beauty shall no more be found;
Nor, in thy marble Vault, shall sound
My ecchoing Song: then Worms shall try
That long preserv'd Virginity:
And your quaint Honour turn to dust;
And into ashes all my Lust.
The Grave's a fine and private place,
But none I think do there embrace.
      Now therefore, while the youthful hew
Sits on thy skin like morning dew,
And while thy willing Soul transpires
At every pore with instant Fires,
Now let us sport us while we may;
And now, like am'rous birds of prey,
Rather at once our Time devour,
Than languish in his slow-chapt pow'r.
Let us roll all our Strength, and all
Our sweetness, up into one Ball:
And tear our Pleasures with rough strife,
Thorough the Iron gates of Life.
Thus, though we cannot make our Sun
Stand still, yet we will make him run.

To the Virgins, to Make Much of Time

ROBERT HERRICK

Gather ye Rose-buds while ye may,
   Old Time is still a flying:
And this same flower that smiles to day,
   To morrow will be dying.

The glorious Lamp of Heaven, the Sun,
   The higher he's a getting;
The sooner will his Race be run,
   And neerer he's to Setting.

That Age is best, which is the first,
   When Youth and Blood are warmer;
But being spent, the worse, and worst
   Times, still succeed the former.

Then be not coy, but use your time;
   And while ye may, goe marry:
For having lost but once your prime,
   You may for ever tarry.

LET ME COUNT THE WAYS:
WORDS OF LOVE

Countless volumes of poetry have been written about those intimate times when the whole world seems to consist of only two people, and 'nothing else is'. These verses are some of the finest, invoking moments of love that last a night, as for Donne, or only a magical hour snatched from the daily grind, as for Duffy. There are as many kinds of love as there are human beings, so the fact that these poems have been adored by generations of readers is testament to their power.

Sonnets from the Portuguese: XLIII

ELIZABETH BARRETT BROWNING

How do I love thee? Let me count the ways.
I love thee to the depth and breadth and height
My soul can reach, when feeling out of sight
For the ends of Being and ideal Grace.
I love thee to the level of everyday's
Most quiet need, by sun and candlelight.
I love thee freely, as men strive for Right;
I love thee purely, as they turn from Praise.
I love thee with the passion put to use
In my old griefs, and with my childhood's faith.
I love thee with a love I seemed to lose
With my lost saints. I love thee with the breath,
Smiles, tears, of all my life; and, if God choose,
I shall but love thee better after death.

A Birthday

CHRISTINA ROSSETTI

My heart is like a singing bird
    Whose nest is in a watered shoot;
My heart is like an apple-tree
    Whose boughs are bent with thickset fruit;
My heart is like a rainbow shell
    That paddles in a halcyon sea;
My heart is gladder than all these,
    Because my love is come to me.

Raise me a dais of silk and down;
    Hang it with vair and purple dyes;
Carve it in doves and pomegranates,
    And peacocks with a hundred eyes;
Work it in gold and silver grapes,
    In leaves and silver fleurs-de-lys;
Because the birthday of my life
    Is come, my love is come to me.

The Sun Rising

JOHN DONNE

Busy old fool, unruly Sun,
    Why dost thou thus,
Through windows and through curtains call on us?
Must to thy motions lovers' seasons run?
    Saucy pedantic wretch, go chide
    Late schoolboys and sour prentices,
  Go tell court-huntsmen that the King will ride,
  Call country ants to harvest offices;
Love, all alike, no season knows nor clime,
Nor hours, days, months, which are the rags of time.

    Thy beams, so reverend and strong
    Why should'st thou think?
I could eclipse and cloud them with a wink,
But that I would not lose her sight so long:
    If her eyes have not blinded thine,
    Look, and tomorrow late, tell me,
  Whether both the Indias of spice and mine
  Be where thou left'st them, or lie here with me.
Ask for those kings whom thou saw'st yesterday,
And thou shalt hear, All here in one bed lay.

She's all states, and all princes, I,
    Nothing else is.
Princes do but play us; compared to this,
All honour's mimic, all wealth alchemy;
    Thou Sun art half as happy as we,
    In that the world's contracted thus.
  Thine age asks ease, and since thy duties be
  To warm the world, that's done in warming us.
Shine here to us, and thou art everywhere;
This bed thy center is, these walls, thy sphere.

Love Song

RAINER MARIA RILKE

When my soul touches yours a great chord sings!
How shall I tune it then to other things?
O! That some spot in darkness could be found
That does not vibrate whene'er your depth sound.
But everything that touches you and me
Welds us as played strings sound one melody.
Where is the instrument whence the sounds flow?
And whose the master-hand that holds the bow?
O! Sweet song –

[translated by Jessie Lemont]

Love Is Not All (Sonnet XXX)

EDNA ST VINCENT MILLAY

Love is not all: it is not meat nor drink
Nor slumber nor a roof against the rain;
Nor yet a floating spar to men that sink
And rise and sink and rise and sink again;
Love can not fill the thickened lung with breath,
Nor clean the blood, nor set the fractured bone;
Yet many a man is making friends with death
Even as I speak, for lack of love alone.
It well may be that in a difficult hour,
Pinned down by pain and moaning for release,
Or nagged by want past resolution's power,
I might be driven to sell your love for peace,
Or trade the memory of this night for food.
It well may be. I do not think I would.

Hour

CAROL ANN DUFFY

Love's time's beggar, but even a single hour,
bright as a dropped coin, makes love rich.
We find an hour together, spend it not on flowers
or wine, but the whole of the summer sky and a grass ditch.

For thousands of seconds we kiss; your hair
like treasure on the ground; the Midas light
turning your limbs to gold. Time slows, for here
we are millionaires, backhanding the night

so nothing dark will end our shining hour,
no jewel hold a candle to the cuckoo spit
hung from the blade of grass at your ear,
no chandelier or spotlight see you better lit

than here. Now. Time hates love, wants love poor,
but love spins gold, gold, gold from straw.

Dover Beach

MATTHEW ARNOLD

The sea is calm to-night.
The tide is full, the moon lies fair
Upon the straits; on the French coast the light
Gleams and is gone; the cliffs of England stand,
Glimmering and vast, out in the tranquil bay.
Come to the window, sweet is the night-air!

Only, from the long line of spray
Where the sea meets the moon-blanch'd land,
Listen! you hear the grating roar
Of pebbles which the waves draw back, and fling,
At their return, up the high strand,
Begin, and cease, and then again begin,
With tremulous cadence slow, and bring
The eternal note of sadness in.

Sophocles long ago
Heard it on the Ægæan, and it brought
Into his mind the turbid ebb and flow
Of human misery; we
Find also in the sound a thought,
Hearing it by this distant northern sea.

The Sea of Faith
Was once, too, at the full, and round earth's shore
Lay like the folds of a bright girdle furl'd.
But now I only hear
Its melancholy, long, withdrawing roar,
Retreating, to the breath
Of the night-wind, down the vast edges drear
And naked shingles of the world.

Ah, love, let us be true
To one another! for the world, which seems
To lie before us like a land of dreams,
So various, so beautiful, so new,
Hath really neither joy, nor love, nor light,
Nor certitude, nor peace, nor help for pain;
And we are here as on a darkling plain
Swept with confused alarms of struggle and flight,
Where ignorant armies clash by night.

THE MARRIAGE OF TRUE MINDS: RELATIONSHIPS

O nce the beloved's heart and hand has been won – and the blood has cooled – a rich seam of poetry provides wisdom on the subject of marriage. In some of these verses wry humour takes the place of breathless passion as the realities of lifelong love sink in. In others, the poet adopts a tone of outright cynicism. Marriage is not the only relationship that has sparked inspiration, though. Friendship – often a less thorny meeting of minds – is also celebrated here in verses by Henry Wadsworth Longfellow and Emily Brontë.

Sonnet 116

WILLIAM SHAKESPEARE

Let me not to the marriage of true mindes
Admit impediments, love is not love
Which alters when it alteration findes,
Or bends with the remover to remove:
O no, it is an ever fixèd marke
That lookes on tempests and is never shaken;
It is the star to every wandring barke,
Whose worths unknowne, although his heigth be taken.
Lov's not Times foole, though rosie lips and cheeks
Within his bending sickles compasse come,
Love alters not with his breefe houres and weekes,
But beares it out even to the edge of doome:
    If this be error, and upon me proved,
    I never writ, nor no man ever love'd.

A Subaltern's Love Song

JOHN BETJEMAN

Miss J. Hunter Dunn, Miss J. Hunter Dunn,
Furnish'd and burnish'd by Aldershot sun,
What strenuous singles we played after tea,
We in the tournament – you against me!

Love-thirty, love-forty, oh! weakness of joy,
The speed of a swallow, the grace of a boy,
With carefullest carelessness, gaily you won,
I am weak from your loveliness, Joan Hunter Dunn.

Miss Joan Hunter Dunn, Miss Joan Hunter Dunn,
How mad I am, sad I am, glad that you won.
The warm-handled racket is back in its press,
But my shock-headed victor, she loves me no less.

Her father's euonymus shines as we walk,
And swing past the summer-house, buried in talk,
And cool the verandah that welcomes us in
To the six-o'clock news and a lime-juice and gin.

The scent of the conifers, sound of the bath,
The view from my bedroom of moss-dappled path,
As I struggle with double-end evening tie,
For we dance at the Golf Club, my victor and I.

On the floor of her bedroom lie blazer and shorts,
And the cream-coloured walls are be-trophied with sports,
And westering, questioning settles the sun,
On your low-leaded window, Miss Joan Hunter Dunn.

The Hillman is waiting, the light's in the hall,
The pictures of Egypt are bright on the wall,
My sweet, I am standing beside the oak stair
And there on the landing's the light on your hair.

By roads 'not adopted', by woodlanded ways,
She drove to the club in the late summer haze,
Into nine-o'clock Camberley, heavy with bells
And mushroomy, pine-woody, evergreen smells.

Miss Joan Hunter Dunn, Miss Joan Hunter Dunn,
I can hear from the car-park the dance has begun,
Oh! full Surrey twilight! importunate band!
Oh! strongly adorable tennis-girl's hand!

Around us are Rovers and Austins afar,
Above us, the intimate roof of the car,
And here on my right is the girl of my choice,
With the tilt of her nose and the chime of her voice,

And the scent of her wrap, and the words never said,
And the ominous, ominous dancing ahead.
We sat in the car park till twenty to one
And now I'm engaged to Miss Joan Hunter Dunn.

A Word to Husbands

OGDEN NASH

To keep your marriage brimming,
With love in the loving cup,
Whenever you're wrong, admit it;
Whenever you're right, shut up.

A Vow

WENDY COPE

I cannot promise never to be angry;
I cannot promise always to be kind.
You know what you are taking on, my darling –
It's only at the start that love is blind.
And yet I'm still the one you want to be with
And you're the one for me – of that I'm sure.
You are my closest friend, my favourite person,
The lover and the home I've waited for.
I cannot promise that I will deserve you
From this day on. I hope to pass that test.
I love you and I want to make you happy.
I promise I will do my very best.

Yes I'll Marry You My Dear

PAM AYRES

Yes, I'll marry you, my dear.
And here's the reason why.
So I can push you out of bed
When the baby starts to cry.
And if we hear a knocking
And it's creepy and it's late,
I hand you the torch you see,
And you investigate.

Yes I'll marry you, my dear,
You may not apprehend it,
But when the tumble-drier goes
It's you that has to mend it.
You have to face the neighbour
Should our labrador attack him,
And if a drunkard fondles me
It's you that has to whack him.

Yes, I'll marry you,
You're virile and you're lean,
My house is like a pigsty
You can help to keep it clean.
That sexy little dinner
Which you served by candlelight,
As I do chipolatas,
You can cook it every night!!!

It's you who has to work the drill
And put up curtain track,
And when I've got PMT it's you who gets the flak,
I do see great advantages,
But none of them for you,
And so before you see the light,
I DO, I DO, I DO!!

Love and Friendship

EMILY BRONTË

Love is like the wild rose-brier;
Friendship like the holly-tree.
The holly is dark when the rose-brier blooms,
But which will bloom most constantly?

The wild rose-brier is sweet in spring,
Its summer blossoms scent the air;
Yet wait till winter comes again,
And who will call the wild-brier fair!

Then, scorn the silly rose-wreath now,
And deck thee with the holly's sheen,
That, when December blights thy brow,
He still may leave thy garland green.

The Arrow and the Song

HENRY WADSWORTH LONGFELLOW

I shot an arrow into the air,
It fell to earth, I knew not where;
For, so swiftly it flew, the sight
Could not follow it in its flight.

I breathed a song into the air,
It fell to earth, I knew not where,
For who has sight so keen and strong,
That it can follow the flight of song?

Long, long afterward, in an oak
I found the arrow, still unbroke,
And the song, from beginning to end,
I found again in the heart of a friend.

Nothing Now Can Ever Come to Any Good: Lost Love and Love Denied

O ne of poetry's greatest comforts is the sensation that others have been tossed on the horns of the same joys and grief that now pierce us. Here are tales of love lost: to another; to the wider world; to death. Wyatt's narrator and the ill-starred Lady of Shalott pine for impossible consummations, while Auden's much-loved 'Funeral Blues' strikes a chord with anyone who has felt bereft. e. e. cummings's words on the acceptance of heartbreak and Derek Walcott's wise advice for building resilience close this chapter with words of comfort.

Funeral Blues

W. H. AUDEN

I

Stop all the clocks, cut off the telephone,
Prevent the dog from barking with a juicy bone,
Silence the pianos and with muffled drum
Bring out the coffin, let the mourners come.

Let aeroplanes circle moaning overhead
Scribbling on the sky the message He Is Dead,
Put crêpe bows round the white necks of the public doves,
Let the traffic policemen wear black cotton gloves.

He was my North, my South, my East and West,
My working week and my Sunday rest,
My noon, my midnight, my talk, my song;
I thought that love would last for ever: I was wrong.

The stars are not wanted now: put out every one;
Pack up the moon and dismantle the sun;
Pour away the ocean and sweep up the wood;
For nothing now can ever come to any good.

The Lady of Shalott [extract]

ALFRED, LORD TENNYSON

Part I

On either side the river lie
Long fields of barley and of rye,
That clothe the wold and meet the sky;
And thro' the field the road runs by
   To many-tower'd Camelot;
And up and down the people go,
Gazing where the lilies blow
Round an island there below,
   The island of Shalott.

Willows whiten, aspens quiver,
Little breezes dusk and shiver
Thro' the wave that runs for ever
By the island in the river
   Flowing down to Camelot.
Four gray walls, and four gray towers,
Overlook a space of flowers,
And the silent isle imbowers
   The Lady of Shalott.

By the margin, willow-veil'd,
Slide the heavy barges trail'd
By slow horses; and unhail'd
The shallop flitteth silken-sail'd
　　Skimming down to Camelot:
But who hath seen her wave her hand?
Or at the casement seen her stand?
Or is she known in all the land,
　　The Lady of Shalott?

Only reapers, reaping early
In among the bearded barley,
Hear a song that echoes cheerly
From the river winding clearly,
　　Down to tower'd Camelot:
And by the moon the reaper weary,
Piling sheaves in uplands airy,
Listening, whispers "Tis the fairy
　　Lady of Shalott."

Part II

There she weaves by night and day
A magic web with colours gay.
She has heard a whisper say,
A curse is on her if she stay
   To look down to Camelot.
She knows not what the curse may be,
And so she weaveth steadily,
And little other care hath she,
   The Lady of Shalott.

And moving thro' a mirror clear
That hangs before her all the year,
Shadows of the world appear.
There she sees the highway near
   Winding down to Camelot:
There the river eddy whirls
And there the surly village-churls,
And the red cloaks of market girls
   Pass onward from Shalott.

Sometimes a troop of damsels glad,
An abbot on an ambling pad,
Sometimes a curly shepherd-lad,
Or long-hair'd page in crimson clad,
   Goes by to tower'd Camelot;
And sometimes thro' the mirror blue
The knights come riding two and two:
She hath no loyal knight and true,
   The Lady of Shalott.

But in her web she still delights
To weave the mirror's magic sights,
For often thro' the silent nights
A funeral, with plumes and lights,
   And music, went to Camelot:
Or when the moon was overhead,
Came two young lovers lately wed;
'I am half sick of shadows,' said
   The Lady of Shalott.

'Who so list to hounte I know where is an hynde'

THOMAS WYATT

Who so list to hounte I know where is an hynde;
    But as for me, helas, I may no more:
    The vayne travaill hath weried me so sore,
    I ame of theim that farthest cometh behinde;
Yet may I by no meanes my weried mynde
    Drawe from the Diere: but as she fleeth afore
    Faynting I folowe; I leve off therefore,
    Sithens in a nett I seke to hold the wynde.
Who list her hount I put him owte of dowbte,
    As well as I may spend his tyme in vain:
    And graven with Diamondes in letters plain
There is written her faier neck rounde abowte:
    Noli me tangere for Cesars I ame,
    And wylde for to hold though I seme tame.'

[after the Italian of Petrarch]

it may not always be so; and i say

e. e. cummings

it may not always be so; and i say
that if your lips, which i have loved, should touch
another's, and your dear strong fingers clutch
his heart, as mine in time not far away;
if on another's face your sweet hair lay
in such silence as i know, or such
great writhing words as, uttering overmuch,
stand helplessly before the spirit at bay;

if this should be, i say if this should be –
you of my heart, send me a little word;
that i may go unto him, and take his hands,
saying, Accept all happiness from me.
Then shall i turn my face, and hear one bird
sing terribly afar in the lost lands.

Love After Love

DEREK WALCOTT

The time will come
when, with elation
you will greet yourself arriving
at your own door, in your own mirror
and each will smile at the other's welcome,

and say, sit here. Eat.
You will love again the stranger who was your self.
Give wine. Give bread. Give back your heart
to itself, to the stranger who has loved you

all your life, whom you ignored
for another, who knows you by heart.
Take down the love letters from the bookshelf,

the photographs, the desperate notes,
peel your own image from the mirror.
Sit. Feast on your life.

Much Have I Travell'd:
Voyages and Antique Lands

A poem can be a portal to adventure and mystery. With a book in our hand, we can be transported from fireside to fairyland and back again in a handful of stanzas. Here is a collection of verses celebrating mythical realms, strange imagined vistas and perilous voyages – as well as a dash of homesickness and a humorous portrait of packing anxiety that anyone who has filled a weekend suitcase will recognise only too well.

The Listeners

WALTER DE LA MARE

'Is there anybody there?' said the Traveller,
    Knocking on the moonlit door;
And his horse in the silence champed the grasses
    Of the forest's ferny floor:
And a bird flew up out of the turret,
    Above the Traveller's head:
And he smote upon the door again a second time;
    'Is there anybody there?' he said.
But no one descended to the Traveller;
    No head from the leaf-fringed sill
Leaned over and looked into his grey eyes,
    Where he stood perplexed and still.
But only a host of phantom listeners
    That dwelt in the lone house then
Stood listening in the quiet of the moonlight
    To that voice from the world of men:
Stood thronging the faint moonbeams on the dark stair,
    That goes down to the empty hall,
Hearkening in an air stirred and shaken
    By the lonely Traveller's call.

And he felt in his heart their strangeness,
    Their stillness answering his cry,
While his horse moved, cropping the dark turf,
    'Neath the starred and leafy sky;
For he suddenly smote on the door, even
    Louder, and lifted his head –
'Tell them I came, and no one answered,
    That I kept my word,' he said.
Never the least stir made the listeners,
    Though every word he spake
Fell echoing through the shadowiness of the still house
    From the one man left awake:
Ay, they heard his foot upon the stirrup,
    And the sound of iron on stone,
And how the silence surged softly backward,
    When the plunging hoofs were gone.

On First Looking into Chapman's Homer

JOHN KEATS

Much have I travelled in the realms of gold,
   And many goodly states and kingdoms seen;
   Round many western islands have I been
Which bards in fealty to Apollo hold.
Oft of one wide expanse had I been told
   That deep-browed Homer ruled as his demesne;
   Yet did I never breathe its pure serene
Till I heard Chapman speak out loud and bold:
Then felt I like some watcher of the skies
   When a new planet swims into his ken;
Or like stout Cortez when with eagle eyes
   He stared at the Pacific – and all his men
Looked at each other with a wild surmise –
   Silent, upon a peak in Darien.

The Solitude of Alexander Selkirk

WILLIAM COWPER

I am monarch of all I survey;
　My right there is none to dispute;
From the centre all round to the sea
　I am lord of the fowl and the brute.
O Solitude! where are the charms
　That sages have seen in thy face?
Better dwell in the midst of alarms,
　Than reign in this horrible place.

I am out of humanity's reach;
　I must finish my journey alone;
Never hear the sweet music of speech;
　I start at the sound of my own.
The beasts that roam over the plain
　My form with indifference see:
They are so unacquainted with man,
　Their tameness is shocking to me.

Society, friendship, and love,
    Divinely bestowed upon man,
O, had I the wings of a dove,
    How soon would I taste you again!
My sorrows I then might assuage
    In the ways of religion and truth;
Might learn from the wisdom of age,
    And be cheered by the sallies of youth.

Religion! what treasure untold
    Resides in that heavenly world!
More precious than silver and gold,
    Or all that this earth can afford.
But the sound of the church-going bell
    These valleys and rocks never heard,
Ne'er sighed at the sound of a knell,
    Or smiled when a Sabbath appeared.

Ye winds that have made me your sport
    Convey to this desolate shore
Some cordial, endearing report
    Of a land I shall visit no more:
My friends, do they now and then send
    A wish or a thought after me?
O, tell me I yet have a friend,
    Though a friend I am never to see.

How fleet is a glance of the mind!
    Compared with the speed of its flight,
The tempest itself lags behind,
    And the swift-wingèd arrows of light.
When I think of my own native land,
    In a moment I seem to be there;
But alas! recollection at hand
    Soon hurries me back to despair.

But the sea-fowl is gone to her nest,
    The beast is laid down in his lair;
Even here is a season of rest,
    And I to my cabin repair.
There's mercy in every place,
    And mercy, encouraging thought!
Gives even affliction a grace,
    And reconciles man to his lot.

Sea-Fever

JOHN MASEFIELD

I must down to the seas again, to the lonely sea and the
    sky,
And all I ask is a tall ship and a star to steer her by,
And the wheel's kick and the wind's song and the white
    sail's shaking,
And a grey mist on the sea's face and a grey dawn
    breaking.

I must down to the seas again, for the call of the running
    tide
Is a wild call and a clear call that may not be denied;
And all I ask is a windy day with the white clouds flying,
And the flung spray and the blown spume, and the
    seagulls crying.

I must down to the seas again, to the vagrant gypsy life,
To the gull's way and the whale's way where the wind's like
    a whetted knife;
And all I ask is a merry yarn from a laughing fellow-rover,
And quiet sleep and a sweet dream when the long trick's
    over.

Far Over the Misty Mountains Cold

J. R. R. TOLKIEN

Far over the misty mountains cold
To dungeons deep and caverns old
We must away ere break of day,
To seek the pale enchanted gold.

The dwarves of yore made mighty spells,
While hammers fell like ringing bells
In places deep, where dark things sleep,
In hollow halls beneath the fells.

For ancient king and elvish lord
There many a gleaming golden hoard
They shaped and wrought, and light they caught
To hide in gems on hilt of sword.

On silver necklaces they strung
The flowering stars, on crowns they hung
The dragon-fire, in twisted wire
They meshed the light of moon and sun.

Far over the misty mountains cold
To dungeons deep and caverns old
We must away ere break of day,
To claim our long-forgotten gold.

Goblets they carved there for themselves
And harps of gold; where no man delves
There lay they long, and many a song
Was sung unheard by men or elves.

The pines were roaring on the height,
The winds were moaning in the night.
The fire was red, it flaming spread;
The trees like torches blazed with light.

The bells were ringing in the dale
And men they looked up with faces pale;
The dragon's ire more fierce than fire
Laid low their towers and houses frail.

The mountain smoked beneath the moon;
The dwarves, they heard the tramp of doom.
They fled their hall to dying fall
Beneath his feet, beneath the moon.

Far over the misty mountains grim
To dungeons deep and caverns dim
We must away ere break of day,
To win our harps and gold from him!

Ozymandias

PERCY BYSSHE SHELLEY

I met a traveller from an antique land
Who said: Two vast and trunkless legs of stone
Stand in the desert . . . Near them, on the sand,
Half sunk, a shattered visage lies, whose frown,
And wrinkled lip, and sneer of cold command,
Tell that its sculptor well those passions read
Which yet survive, stamped on these lifeless things,
The hand that mocked them, and the heart that fed:
And on the pedestal these words appear:
'My name is Ozymandias, king of kings:
Look on my works, ye Mighty, and despair!'
Nothing beside remains. Round the decay
Of that colossal wreck, boundless and bare
The lone and level sands stretch far away.

Kubla Khan

SAMUEL TAYLOR COLERIDGE

In Xanadu did Kubla Khan
A stately pleasure-dome decree:
Where Alph, the sacred river, ran
Through caverns measureless to man
   Down to a sunless sea.
So twice five miles of fertile ground
With walls and towers were girdled round:
And there were gardens bright with sinuous rills,
Where blossomed many an incense-bearing tree;
And here were forests ancient as the hills,
Enfolding sunny spots of greenery.
But oh! that deep romantic chasm which slanted
Down the green hill athwart a cedarn cover!
A savage place! as holy and enchanted
As e'er beneath a waning moon was haunted
By woman wailing for her demon-lover!
And from this chasm, with ceaseless turmoil seething,
As if this earth in fast thick pants were breathing,
A mighty fountain momently was forced:
Amid whose swift half-intermitted burst
Huge fragments vaulted like rebounding hail,

Or chaffy grain beneath the thresher's flail:
And 'mid these dancing rocks at once and ever
It flung up momently the sacred river.
Five miles meandering with a mazy motion
Through wood and dale the sacred river ran,
Then reached the caverns measureless to man,
And sank in tumult to a lifeless ocean:
And 'mid this tumult Kubla heard from far
Ancestral voices prophesying war!
    The shadow of the dome of pleasure
    Floated midway on the waves;
    Where was heard the mingled measure
    From the fountain and the caves.
It was a miracle of rare device,
A sunny pleasure-dome with caves of ice!

    A damsel with a dulcimer
    In a vision once I saw:
    It was an Abyssinian maid,
    And on her dulcimer she played,
    Singing of Mount Abora.
    Could I revive within me
    Her symphony and song,
    To such a deep delight 'twould win me,

That with music loud and long,
I would build that dome in air,
That sunny dome! those caves of ice!
And all who heard should see them there,
And all should cry, Beware! Beware!
His flashing eyes, his floating hair!
Weave a circle round him thrice,
And close your eyes with holy dread,
For he on honey-dew hath fed,
And drunk the milk of Paradise.

Home-Thoughts, from Abroad

ROBERT BROWNING

Oh, to be in England
Now that April's there,
And whoever wakes in England
Sees, some morning, unaware,
That the lowest boughs and the brushwood sheaf
Round the elm-tree bole are in tiny leaf,
While the chaffinch sings on the orchard bough
In England – now!

And after April, when May follows,
And the whitethroat builds, and all the swallows!
Hark, where my blossomed pear-tree in the hedge
Leans to the field and scatters on the clover
Blossoms and dewdrops – at the bent spray's edge –
That's the wise thrush; he sings each song twice over,
Lest you should think he never could recapture
The first fine careless rapture!
And though the fields look rough with hoary dew,
All will be gay when noontide wakes anew
The buttercups, the little children's dower
– Far brighter than this gaudy melon-flower!

Just in Case

CHARLOTTE MITCHELL

I'm going to the sea for the weekend,
in a couple of days I'll be back,
so I'll just take my little brown suit and a blouse
and a beret and carry my mac.

But what if the house is a cold one,
the house where I'm going to stay,
no fires after April, no hot drinks at night
and the windows wide open all day?
I'd better take one – no, *two* cardys
and my long tartan scarf for my head,
and my chaste new pyjamas in case they decide
to bring me my breakfast in bed.
And what about church on the Sunday?
I could wear my beret and suit,
but if it were sunny, it would be a chance
to wear my straw hat with the fruit.
I can't wear my little brown suit, though,
not with the straw with the fruit,
so I'll just take a silk dress to go with the straw
and a silk scarf to go with the suit.

I'll just take my jeans and that jumper
in case we go out in a car,
and my Guernsey in case we go out in a boat
and d'you know where my swimming things are?

D'you think I should take that black velvet
in case they've booked seats for a play?
And is it still usual to take your own towel
when you go somewhere to stay?
I had thought of just taking slippers,
but they do look disgustingly old,
I'd better take best shoes and sandals and boots
for the church and the heat and the cold.

I daren't go without my umbrella
in case I'm dressed up and it rains;
I'm bound to need socks and my wellies
for walking down long muddy lanes.

I'd rather not take my old dressing-gown,
it is such a business to pack,
but 'spose they have breakfast before they get dressed
I'd have to have mine in my mac.

I'm going to the sea for the weekend,
in a couple of days I'll be back,
so I'll just take my little brown suit and a blouse,
    two cardys, my long tartan scarf,
    my chaste new pyjamas,
    my straw hat with the fruit,
    my silk dress, my silk scarf,
    my jeans, that jumper,
    my Guernsey, my swimming things,
    my black velvet, my towel, my
    slippers (no one need see them)
    my sandals, my boots, my
    umbrella, my socks, my wellies,
    my dressing-gown, no, not
    my dressing-gown, OK my
    dressing-gown
and a beret and carry my mac.

FROM WILD THINGS TO WESTMINSTER: FINDING POETRY IN TOWN AND COUNTRY

The pleasures of the natural world have inspired many of our most loved poems. Even before the Romantics started chasing the sublime across moors and mountains, the pastoral tradition had long fêted rural delights. We can benefit from the restorative powers of nature – whether savoured in the wood's green heart or enjoyed as it flashes past train windows – in the space of a few airy lines. As this selection proves, though, poets have not only been moved by bucolic scenes: even Wordsworth, laureate of the Lakes, found his heart sent soaring by the urban splendour of a Westminster morning.

The Peace of Wild Things

WENDELL BERRY

When despair for the world grows in me
and I wake in the night at the least sound
in fear of what my life and my children's lives may be,
I go and lie down where the wood drake
rests in his beauty on the water, and the great heron feeds.
I come into the peace of wild things
who do not tax their lives with forethought
of grief. I come into the presence of still water.
And I feel above me the day-blind stars
waiting with their light. For a time
I rest in the grace of the world, and am free.

I Wandered Lonely as a Cloud

WILLIAM WORDSWORTH

I wandered lonely as a cloud
That floats on high o'er vales and hills,
When all at once I saw a crowd,
A host, of golden daffodils;
Beside the lake, beneath the trees,
Fluttering and dancing in the breeze.

Continuous as the stars that shine
And twinkle on the milky way,
They stretched in never-ending line
Along the margin of a bay:
Ten thousand saw I at a glance,
Tossing their heads in sprightly dance.

The waves beside them danced; but they
Out-did the sparkling waves in glee:
A poet could not but be gay,
In such a jocund company:
I gazed – and gazed – but little thought
What wealth the show to me had brought:

For oft, when on my couch I lie
In vacant or in pensive mood,
They flash upon that inward eye
Which is the bliss of solitude;
And then my heart with pleasure fills,
And dances with the daffodils.

To A Fat Lady Seen From the Train

FRANCES CORNFORD

O why do you walk through the fields in gloves,
    Missing so much and so much?
O fat white woman whom nobody loves,
Why do you walk through the fields in gloves,
When the grass is soft as the breast of doves
    And shivering-sweet to the touch?
O why do you walk through the fields in gloves,
    Missing so much and so much?

The Way Through the Woods

RUDYARD KIPLING

They shut the road through the woods
Seventy years ago.
Weather and rain have undone it again,
And now you would never know
There was once a road through the woods
Before they planted the trees.
It is underneath the coppice and heath,
And the thin anemones.
Only the keeper sees
That, where the ring-dove broods,
And the badgers roll at ease,
There was once a road through the woods.

Yet, if you enter the woods
Of a summer evening late,
When the night-air cools on the trout-ringed pools
Where the otter whistles his mate,
(They fear not men in the woods,
Because they see so few)
You will hear the beat of a horse's feet,
And the swish of a skirt in the dew,

Steadily cantering through
The misty solitudes,
As though they perfectly knew
The old lost road through the woods . . .
But there is no road through the woods.

Fog

CARL SANDBURG

The fog comes
on little cat feet.

It sits looking
over harbor and city
on silent haunches
and then moves on.

Loveliest of trees, the cherry now

A. E. HOUSMAN

Loveliest of trees, the cherry now
Is hung with bloom along the bough,
And stands about the woodland ride
Wearing white for Eastertide.

Now, of my threescore years and ten,
Twenty will not come again,
And take from seventy springs a score,
It only leaves me fifty more.

And since to look at things in bloom
Fifty springs are little room,
About the woodlands I will go
To see the cherry hung with snow.

The Lake Isle of Innisfree

WILLIAM BUTLER YEATS

I will arise and go now, and go to Innisfree,
And a small cabin build there, of clay and wattles made;
Nine bean-rows will I have there, a hive for the honey-bee,
And live alone in the bee-loud glade.

And I shall have some peace there, for peace comes
dropping slow,
Dropping from the veils of the morning to where the
cricket sings;
There midnight's all a glimmer, and noon a purple glow,
And evening full of the linnet's wings.

I will arise and go now, for always night and day
I hear lake water lapping with low sounds by the shore;
While I stand on the roadway, or on the pavements grey,
I hear it in the deep heart's core.

Leisure

W. H. DAVIES

What is this life if, full of care,
We have no time to stand and stare.

No time to stand beneath the boughs
And stare as long as sheep and cows.

No time to see, when woods we pass,
Where squirrels hide their nuts in grass.

No time to see, in broad daylight,
Streams full of stars, like skies at night.

No time to turn at Beauty's glance,
And watch her feet, how they can dance.

No time to wait till her mouth can
Enrich that smile her eyes began.

A poor life this if, full of care,
We have no time to stand and stare.

Stopping by Woods on a Snowy Evening

ROBERT FROST

Whose woods these are I think I know.
His house is in the village though;
He will not see me stopping here
To watch his woods fill up with snow.

My little horse must think it queer
To stop without a farmhouse near
Between the woods and frozen lake
The darkest evening of the year.

He gives his harness bells a shake
To ask if there is some mistake.
The only other sound's the sweep
Of easy wind and downy flake.

The woods are lovely, dark and deep.
But I have promises to keep,
And miles to go before I sleep,
And miles to go before I sleep.

The Tables Turned

WILLIAM WORDSWORTH

Up! up! my Friend, and quit your books;
Or surely you'll grow double:
Up! up! my Friend, and clear your looks;
Why all this toil and trouble?

The sun, above the mountain's head,
A freshening lustre mellow
Through all the long green fields has spread,
His first sweet evening yellow.

Books! 'tis a dull and endless strife:
Come, hear the woodland linnet,
How sweet his music! on my life,
There's more of wisdom in it.

And hark! how blithe the throstle sings!
He, too, is no mean preacher:
Come forth into the light of things,
Let Nature be your Teacher.

She has a world of ready wealth,
Our minds and hearts to bless –
Spontaneous wisdom breathed by health,
Truth breathed by cheerfulness.

One impulse from a vernal wood
May teach you more of man,
Of moral evil and of good,
Than all the sages can.

Sweet is the lore which Nature brings;
Our meddling intellect
Mis-shapes the beauteous forms of things: –
We murder to dissect.

Enough of Science and of Art;
Close up those barren leaves;
Come forth, and bring with you a heart
That watches and receives.

Blackberry-Picking

SEAMUS HEANEY

For Philip Hobsbaum

Late August, given heavy rain and sun
For a full week, the blackberries would ripen.
At first, just one, a glossy purple clot
Among others, red, green, hard as a knot.
You ate that first one and its flesh was sweet
Like thickened wine: summer's blood was in it
Leaving stains upon the tongue and lust for
Picking. Then red ones inked up and that hunger
Sent us out with milk-cans, pea-tins, jam-pots
Where briars scratched and wet grass bleached our boots.
Round hayfields, cornfields and potato-drills
We trekked and picked until the cans were full,
Until the tinkling bottom had been covered
With green ones, and on top big dark blobs burned
Like a plate of eyes. Our hands were peppered
With thorn pricks, our palms sticky as Bluebeard's.

We hoarded the fresh berries in the byre.
But when the bath was filled we found a fur,
A rat-grey fungus, glutting on our cache.
The juice was stinking too. Once off the bush
The fruit fermented, the sweet flesh would turn sour.
I always felt like crying. It wasn't fair
That all the lovely canfuls smelt of rot.
Each year I hoped they'd keep, knew they would not.

Composed Upon Westminster Bridge, September 3, 1802

WILLIAM WORDSWORTH

Earth has not anything to show more fair:
Dull would he be of soul who could pass by
A sight so touching in its majesty:
This City now doth, like a garment, wear
The beauty of the morning; silent, bare,
Ships, towers, domes, theatres, and temples lie
Open unto the fields, and to the sky;
All bright and glittering in the smokeless air.
Never did sun more beautifully steep
In his first splendour, valley, rock, or hill;
Ne'er saw I, never felt, a calm so deep!
The river glideth at his own sweet will:
Dear God! the very houses seem asleep;
And all that mighty heart is lying still!

Caterpillars and Cats are Lively and Excellent Puns: Birds and Beasts

These poems celebrate animals from the snail to the elephant, and consider the beauties of all kinds of birds and beasts. It has always been a favourite poetic game to imagine their preoccupations and give voice to their mysterious thoughts especially, though not exclusively, in works aimed at young readers. Anyone who has been thrilled by the sight of birds in flight, or subject to the haughty glare of an inscrutable cat, will find much to enjoy here. Many of these verses also consider the divine, since writers throughout the centuries have seen the fingerprints of a holy creator on the animals that share our world.

Ducks

F. W. HARVEY

I

From troubles of the world
I turn to ducks,
Beautiful comical things
Sleeping or curled
Their heads beneath white wings
By water cool,
Or finding curious things
To eat in various mucks
Beneath the pool,
Tails uppermost, or waddling
Sailor-like on the shores
Of ponds, or paddling
Left! Right! – with fanlike feet
Which are for steady oars
When they (white galleys) float
Each bird a boat
Rippling at will the sweet
Wide waterway . . .
When night is fallen *you* creep

Upstairs, but drakes and dillies
Nest with pale water-stars,
Moonbeams and shadow bars,
And water-lilies:
Fearful too much to sleep
Since they've no locks
To click against the teeth
Of weasel and fox.
And warm beneath
Are eggs of cloudy green
Whence hungry rats and lean
Would stealthily suck
New life, but for the mien
The bold ferocious mien
Of the mother-duck.

II

Yes, ducks are valiant things
On nests of twigs and straws,
And ducks are soothy things
And lovely on the lake
When that the sunlight draws
Thereon their pictures dim
In colours cool.

And when beneath the pool
They dabble, and when they swim
And make their rippling rings,
O ducks are beautiful things!
But ducks are comical things: –
As comical as you.
Quack!
They waddle round, they do.
They eat all sorts of things,
And then they quack.
By barn and stable and stack
They wander at their will,
But if you go too near
They look at you through black
Small topaz-tinted eyes
And wish you ill.
Triangular and clear
They leave their curious track
In mud at the water's edge,
And there amid the sedge
And slime they gobble and peer
Saying 'Quack! Quack!'

III

When God had finished the stars and whirl of coloured
    suns
He turned His mind from big things to fashion little ones;
Beautiful tiny things (like daisies) He made, and then
He made the comical ones in case the minds of men
Should stiffen and become
Dull, humourless and glum,
And so forgetful of their Maker be
As to take even themselves – *quite seriously.*
Caterpillars and cats are lively and excellent puns:
All God's jokes are good – even the practical ones!
And as for the duck, I think God must have smiled a bit
Seeing those bright eyes blink on the day He fashioned it.
And He's probably laughing still at the sound that came
    out of its bill!

The Naming of Cats

T. S. ELIOT

The Naming of Cats is a difficult matter,
    It isn't just one of your holiday games;
You may think at first I'm as mad as a hatter
    When I tell you, a cat must have THREE DIFFERENT
    NAMES.
First of all, there's the name that the family use daily,
    Such as Peter, Augustus, Alonzo, or James,
Such as Victor or Jonathan, George or Bill Bailey –
    All of them sensible everyday names.
There are fancier names if you think they sound sweeter,
    Some for the gentlemen, some for the dames:
Such as Plato, Admetus, Electra, Demeter –
    But all of them sensible everyday names.
But I tell you, a cat needs a name that's particular,
    A name that's peculiar, and more dignified,
Else how can he keep up his tail perpendicular,
    Or spread out his whiskers, or cherish his pride?
Of names of this kind, I can give you a quorum,
    Such as Munkstrap, Quaxo, or Coricopat,
Such as Bombalurina, or else Jellylorum –
    Names that never belong to more than one cat.
But above and beyond there's still one name left over,
    And that is the name that you never will guess;

The name that no human research can discover –
    But THE CAT HIMSELF KNOWS, and will never confess.
When you notice a cat in profound meditation,
    The reason, I tell you, is always the same:
His mind is engaged in a rapt contemplation
    Of the thought, of the thought, of the thought of his
        name:
        His ineffable effable
        Effanineffable
Deep and inscrutable singular Name.

The Windhover

GERARD MANLEY HOPKINS

To Christ our Lord

I caught this morning morning's minion, kingdom of
    daylight's dauphin, dapple-dawn-drawn Falcon, in his
    riding
  Of the rolling level underneath him steady air, and
      striding
High there, how he rung upon the rein of a wimpling wing
In his ecstasy! then off, off forth on swing,
  As a skate's heel sweeps smooth on a bow-bend: the hurl
    and gliding
  Rebuffed the big wind. My heart in hiding
Stirred for a bird, – the achieve of; the mastery of the
    thing!

Brute beauty and valour and act, oh, air, pride, plume, here
  Buckle! AND the fire that breaks from thee then, a
    billion
Times told lovelier, more dangerous, O my chevalier!

  No wonder of it: shéer plód makes plough down sillion
Shine, and blue-bleak embers, ah my dear,
  Fall, gall themselves, and gash gold-vermilion.

The Lamb

WILLIAM BLAKE

Little lamb, who made thee?
Dost thou know who made thee,
Gave thee life, and bid thee feed
By the stream and o'er the mead;
Gave thee clothing of delight,
Softest clothing, wooly, bright;
Gave thee such a tender voice,
Making all the vales rejoice?
Little lamb who made thee?
Dost thou know who made thee?

Little lamb I'll tell thee,
Little lamb I'll tell thee:
He is callèd by thy name,
For He calls Himself a Lamb.
He is meek, and He is mild;
He became a little child.
I a child, and thou a lamb,
We are callèd by His name.
Little lamb, God bless thee!
Little lamb, God bless thee!

Adlestrop

EDWARD THOMAS

Yes. I remember Adlestrop –
The name, because one afternoon
Of heat the express-train drew up there
Unwontedly. It was late June.

The steam hissed. Someone cleared his throat.
No one left and no one came
On the bare platform. What I saw
Was Adlestrop – only the name

And willows, willow-herb, and grass,
And meadowsweet, and haycocks dry,
No whit less still and lonely fair
Than the high cloudlets in the sky.

And for that minute a blackbird sang
Close by, and round him, mistier,
Farther and farther, all the birds
Of Oxfordshire and Gloucestershire.

Considering the Snail

THOM GUNN

The snail pushes through a green
night, for the grass is heavy
with water and meets over
the bright path he makes, where rain
has darkened the earth's dark. He
moves in a wood of desire,

pale antlers barely stirring
as he hunts. I cannot tell
what power is at work, drenched there
with purpose, knowing nothing.
What is a snail's fury? All
I think is that if later

I parted the blades above
the tunnel and saw the thin
trail of broken white across
litter, I would never have
imagined the slow passion
to that deliberate progress.

Answer to a Child's Question

SAMUEL TAYLOR COLERIDGE

Do you ask what the birds say? The sparrow, the dove,
The linnet and thrush say, 'I love and I love!'
In the winter they're silent – the wind is so strong;
What it says, I don't know, but it sings a loud song.
But green leaves, and blossoms, and sunny warm weather,
And singing, and loving – all come back together.
But the lark is so brimful of gladness and love,
The green fields below him, the blue sky above,
That he sings, and he sings; and for ever sings he –
'I love my Love, and my Love loves me!'

Pied Beauty

GERARD MANLEY HOPKINS

Glory be to God for dappled things –
   For skies of couple-colour as a brinded cow;
     For rose-moles all in stipple upon trout that swim;
Fresh-firecoal chestnut-falls; finches' wings;
   Landscape plotted and pieced – fold, fallow, and plough;
     And áll trádes, their gear and tackle and trim.

All things counter, original, spare, strange;
   Whatever is fickle, freckled (who knows how?)
     With swift, slow; sweet, sour; adazzle, dim;
He fathers-forth whose beauty is past change:
                  Praise him.

The Tyger

WILLIAM BLAKE

Tyger Tyger, burning bright,
In the forests of the night:
What immortal hand or eye,
Could frame thy fearful symmetry?

In what distant deeps or skies
Burnt the fire of thine eyes!
On what wings dare he aspire?
What the hand, dare sieze the fire?

And what shoulder, and what art,
Could twist the sinews of thy heart?
And when thy heart began to beat,
What dread hand? and what dread feet?

What the hammer? what the chain,
In what furnace was thy brain?
What the anvil? what dread grasp,
Dare its deadly terrors clasp?

When the stars threw down their spears
And water'd heaven with their tears:
Did he smile his work to see?
Did he who made the Lamb make thee?

Tyger, Tyger burning bright,
In the forests of the night:
What immortal hand or eye,
Dare frame thy fearful symmetry?

The Elephant

HILAIRE BELLOC

When people call this beast to mind,
 They marvel more and more
At such a LITTLE tail behind,
 So LARGE a trunk before.

There is Another Sky:
Gods and Heavens

From the ecstatic revelation granted to a young pilot to the wry observations of Betjeman's terribly Anglican church mouse, theology has proved endlessly thought-provoking for poets. In every language and from the earliest times, writers have probed and praised their relationship with the holy. Many of us learned psalms, hymns and carols in early childhood, and we carry those words with us throughout life, whatever our beliefs. The poems in this chapter, whether expressions of doubt or devotion, join that canon.

There Is Another Sky

EMILY DICKINSON

There is another sky,
Ever serene and fair,
And there is another sunshine,
Though it be darkness there;
Never mind faded forests, Austin,
Never mind silent fields –
Here is a little forest,
Whose leaf is ever green;
Here is a brighter garden,
Where not a frost has been;
In its unfading flowers
I hear the bright bee hum;
Prithee, my brother,
Into *my* garden come!

Milton

[extract]

WILLIAM BLAKE

And did those feet in ancient time
Walk upon Englands mountains green:
And was the holy Lamb of God,
On Englands pleasant pastures seen!

And did the Countenance Divine,
Shine forth upon our clouded hills?
And was Jerusalem builded here,
Among these dark Satanic Mills?

Bring me my Bow of burning gold:
Bring me my Arrows of desire:
Bring me my Spear: O clouds unfold!
Bring me my Chariot of fire!

I will not cease from Mental Fight,
Nor shall my Sword sleep in my hand:
Till we have built Jerusalem,
In Englands green and pleasant Land.

Diary of a Church Mouse

JOHN BETJEMAN

Here among long-discarded cassocks,
Damp stools, and half-split open hassocks,
Here where the Vicar never looks
I nibble through old service books.
Lean and alone I spend my days
Behind this Church of England baize.
I share my dark forgotten room
With two oil-lamps and half a broom.
The cleaner never bothers me,
So here I eat my frugal tea.
My bread is sawdust mixed with straw;
My jam is polish for the floor.

　　Christmas and Easter may be feasts
For congregations and for priests,
And so may Whitsun. All the same,
They do not fill my meagre frame.
For me the only feast at all
Is Autumn's Harvest Festival,
When I can satisfy my want
With ears of corn around the font.
I climb the eagle's brazen head
To burrow through a loaf of bread.

I scramble up the pulpit stair
And gnaw the marrows hanging there.
  It is enjoyable to taste
These items ere they go to waste,
But how annoying when one finds
That other mice with pagan minds
Come into church my food to share
Who have no proper business there.
Two field mice who have no desire
To be baptized, invade the choir.
A large and most unfriendly rat
Comes in to see what we are at.
He says he thinks there is no God
And yet he comes ... it's rather odd.
This year he stole a sheaf of wheat
(It screened our special preacher's seat),
And prosperous mice from fields away
Come in to hear the organ play,
And under cover of its notes
Ate through the altar's sheaf of oats.
A Low Church mouse, who thinks that I
Am too papistical, and High,
Yet somehow doesn't think it wrong
To munch through Harvest Evensong,
While I, who starve the whole year through,
Must share my food with rodents who

Except at this time of the year
Not once inside the church appear.

　Within the human world I know
Such goings-on could not be so,
For human beings only do
What their religion tells them to.
They read the Bible every day
And always, night and morning, pray,
And just like me, the good church mouse,
Worship each week in God's own house,

　But all the same it's strange to me
How very full the church can be
With people I don't see at all
Except at Harvest Festival.

Pippa's Song

ROBERT BROWNING

The year's at the spring,
And day's at the morn;
Morning's at seven;
The hill-side's dew-pearl'd;
The lark's on the wing;
The snail's on the thorn;
God's in His heaven –
All's right with the world!

High Flight

JOHN GILLESPIE MAGEE

Oh! I have slipped the surly bonds of Earth
And danced the skies on laughter-silvered wings;
Sunward I've climbed, and joined the tumbling mirth
Of sun-split clouds, – and done a hundred things
You have not dreamed of – wheeled and soared and swung
High in the sunlit silence. Hov'ring there,
I've chased the shouting wind along, and flung
My eager craft through footless halls of air . . .

Up, up the long, delirious, burning blue
I've topped the wind-swept heights with easy grace,
Where never lark, or even eagle flew –
And, while with silent, lifting mind I've trod
The high untrespassed sanctity of space,
Put out my hand, and touched the face of God.

Psalm 23: The Lord Is My Shepherd
A PSALM OF DAVID [FROM THE KING JAMES BIBLE]

The LORD is my shepherd; I shall not want.

He maketh me to lie down in green pastures: he leadeth
me beside the still waters.

He restoreth my soul: he leadeth me in the paths of
righteousness for his name's sake.

Yea, though I walk through the valley of the shadow of
death, I will fear no evil: for thou art with me; thy rod
and thy staff they comfort me.

Thou preparest a table before me in the presence of mine
enemies: thou annointest my head with oil; my cup
runneth over.

Surely goodness and mercy shall follow me all the days of
my life: and I will dwell in the house of the LORD for
ever.

THE GREAT HOUR OF DESTINY:
SONGS OF WAR

Bards had always celebrated heroic
warriors and depicted the fury of battle,
but the flood of poetry that emerged from the
trenches of the First World War made perhaps
the greatest impact on the genre. Thousands
of poems – some brilliantly written and many
less so – were produced by soldiers processing
their extreme experiences. Poets including
Wilfred Owen and Siegfried Sassoon, who
gave harrowing insights into the realities
endured by the troops, achieved popularity
after the event. It is these poems – rather
than the patriotic output of writers such as
Rupert Brooke – that are today perceived as
the authentic voice of that conflict, setting the
tone for much war poetry to follow.

Dreamers

SIEGFRIED SASSOON

Soldiers are citizens of death's grey land,
    Drawing no dividend from time's to-morrows.
In the great hour of destiny they stand,
    Each with his feuds, and jealousies, and sorrows
Soldiers are sworn to action; they must win
    Some flaming, fatal climax with their lives.
Soldiers are dreamers; when the guns begin
    They think of firelit homes, clean beds and wives.

I see them in foul dug-outs, gnawed by rats,
    And in the ruined trenches, lashed with rain,
Dreaming of things they did with balls and bats,
    And mocked by hopeless longing to regain
Bank-holidays, and picture shows, and spats,
    And going to the office in the train.

Strange Meeting

WILFRED OWEN

It seemed that out of battle I escaped
Down some profound dull tunnel, long since scooped
Through granites which titanic wars had groined.

Yet also there encumbered sleepers groaned,
Too fast in thought or death to be bestirred.
Then, as I probed them, one sprang up, and stared
With piteous recognition in fixed eyes,
Lifting distressful hands, as if to bless.
And by his smile, I knew that sullen hall, –
By his dead smile I knew we stood in Hell.

With a thousand pains that vision's face was grained;
Yet no blood reached there from the upper ground,
And no guns thumped, or down the flues made moan.
'Strange friend,' I said, 'here is no cause to mourn.'
'None,' said that other, 'save the undone years,
The hopelessness. Whatever hope is yours,
Was my life also; I went hunting wild
After the wildest beauty in the world,
Which lies not calm in eyes, or braided hair,
But mocks the steady running of the hour,

And if it grieves, grieves richlier than here.
For by my glee might many men have laughed,
And of my weeping something had been left,
Which must die now. I mean the truth untold,
The pity of war, the pity war distilled.
Now men will go content with what we spoiled.
Or, discontent, boil bloody, and be spilled.
They will be swift with swiftness of the tigress.
None will break ranks, though nations trek from progress.
Courage was mine, and I had mystery,
Wisdom was mine, and I had mastery:
To miss the march of this retreating world
Into vain citadels that are not walled.
Then, when much blood had clogged their chariot-wheels,
I would go up and wash them from sweet wells,
Even with truths that lie too deep for taint.
I would have poured my spirit without stint
But not through wounds; not on the cess of war.
Foreheads of men have bled where no wounds were.

'I am the enemy you killed, my friend.
I knew you in this dark: for so you frowned
Yesterday through me as you jabbed and killed.
I parried; but my hands were loath and cold.
Let us sleep now . . .'

Bloody Orkney

HAMISH BLAIR

[This poem is often attributed to a naval officer stationed
in Orkney during the Second World War.]

This bloody town's a bloody cuss
No bloody trains, no bloody bus,
And no one cares for bloody us
In bloody Orkney.

The bloody roads are bloody bad,
The bloody folks are bloody mad,
They'd make the brightest bloody sad,
In bloody Orkney.

All bloody clouds, and bloody rains,
No bloody kerbs, no bloody drains,
The Council's got no bloody brains,
In bloody Orkney.

Everything's so bloody dear,
A bloody bob, for bloody beer,
And is it good? – no bloody fear,
In bloody Orkney.

The bloody 'flicks' are bloody old,
The bloody seats are bloody cold,
You can't get in for bloody gold
In bloody Orkney.

The bloody dances make you smile,
The bloody band is bloody vile,
It only cramps your bloody style,
In bloody Orkney.

No bloody sport, no bloody games,
No bloody fun, the bloody dames
Won't even give their bloody names
In bloody Orkney.

Best bloody place is bloody bed,
With bloody ice on bloody head,
You might as well be bloody dead,
In bloody Orkney.

There's nothing greets your bloody eye
But bloody sea and bloody sky,
'Roll on demob!' we bloody cry
In bloody Orkney.

The Soldier

RUPERT BROOKE

If I should die, think only this of me:
    That there's some corner of a foreign field
That is for ever England. There shall be
    In that rich earth a richer dust concealed;
A dust whom England bore, shaped, made aware,
    Gave, once, her flowers to love, her ways to roam,
A body of England's, breathing English air,
    Washed by the rivers, blest by suns of home.

And think, this heart, all evil shed away,
    A pulse in the eternal mind, no less
        Gives somewhere back the thoughts by England
            given;
Her sights and sounds; dreams happy as her day;
    And laughter, learnt of friends; and gentleness,
        In hearts at peace, under an English heaven.

In Flanders' Fields

JOHN MCCRAE

In Flanders' fields the poppies blow
Between the crosses, row on row,
That mark our place; and in the sky
The larks, still bravely singing, fly
Scarce heard amid the guns below.

We are the Dead. Short days ago
We lived, felt dawn, saw sunset glow,
Loved and were loved, and now we lie
In Flanders' fields.

Take up our quarrel with the foe:
To you from failing hands we throw
The torch; be yours to hold it high.
If ye break faith with us who die
We shall not sleep, though poppies grow
In Flanders' fields.

The Charge of the Light Brigade

ALFRED, LORD TENNYSON

Half a league, half a league,
   Half a league onward,
All in the valley of Death
   Rode the six hundred.
'Forward, the Light Brigade!
Charge for the guns!' he said:
Into the valley of Death
   Rode the six hundred.

'Forward, the Light Brigade!'
Was there a man dismay'd?
Not tho' the soldier knew
   Some one had blunder'd:
Their's not to make reply,
Their's not to reason why,
Their's but to do and die.
Into the valley of Death
   Rode the six hundred.

Cannon to right of them,
Cannon to left of them,
Cannon in front of them
    Volley'd and thunder'd;
Storm'd at with shot and shell,
Boldly they rode and well,
Into the jaws of Death,
Into the mouth of Hell
    Rode the six hundred.

Flash'd all their sabres bare,
Flash'd as they turn'd in air
Sabring the gunners there,
Charging an army, while
    All the world wonder'd:
Plunged in the battery-smoke
Right thro' the line they broke;
Cossack and Russian
Reel'd from the sabre-stroke
    Shatter'd and sunder'd.
Then they rode back, but not
    Not the six hundred.

Cannon to right of them,
Cannon to left of them,
Cannon behind them
　　Volley'd and thunder'd;
Storm'd at with shot and shell,
While horse and hero fell,
They that had fought so well
Came thro' the jaws of Death,
Back from the mouth of Hell,
All that was left of them,
　　Left of six hundred.

When can their glory fade?
O the wild charge they made!
　　All the world wonder'd.
Honour the charge they made!
Honour the Light Brigade,
　　Noble six hundred!

The Dying of the Light:
Elegies and Epitaphs

It would be fair to accuse poets of being a fairly morbid bunch, since death as a preoccupation frequently creeps into verses that take love, or nature, or any number of other subjects as their ostensible theme. Some of the most moving and memorable poetry sees a writer dissecting the irresistible mystery of death, or eulogising a departed beloved. The comfort in reading these verses and knowing that others have endured and survived great grief is one of poetry's greatest consolations.

Do Not Go Gentle into that Good Night

DYLAN THOMAS

Do not go gentle into that good night,
Old age should burn and rave at close of day;
Rage, rage against the dying of the light.

Though wise men at their end know dark is right,
Because their words had forked no lightning they
Do not go gentle into that good night.

Good men, the last wave by, crying how bright
Their frail deeds might have danced in a green bay,
Rage, rage against the dying of the light.

Wild men who caught and sang the sun in flight,
And learn, too late, they grieved it on its way,
Do not go gentle into that good night.

Grave men, near death, who see with blinding sight
Blind eyes could blaze like meteors and be gay,
Rage, rage against the dying of the light.

And you, my father, there on the sad height,
Curse, bless, me now with your fierce tears, I pray.
Do not go gentle into that good night.
Rage, rage against the dying of the light.

A Vision upon this Conceit of
The Faerie Queene

SIR WALTER RALEIGH

[Written in response to Edmund Spenser's
incomplete poem *The Faerie Queene*.]

Methought I saw the grave where Laura lay
Within that temple where the vestal flame
Was wont to burn: and, passing by that way,
To see that buried dust of living fame,
Whose tomb fair Love and fairer Virtue kept,
All suddenly I saw the Fairy Queen,
At whose approach the soul of Petrarch wept;
And from thenceforth those Graces were not seen,
For they this Queen attended; in whose stead
Oblivion laid him down on Laura's hearse.
Hereat the hardest stones were seen to bleed,
And groans of buried ghosts the heavens did pierce:
    Where Homer's spright did tremble all for grief,
    And curs'd th' access of that celestial thief.

Elegy Written in a Country Church Yard
[extract]
THOMAS GRAY

The Curfew tolls the knell of parting day,
The lowing herd wind slowly o'er the lea,
The plowman homeward plods his weary way,
And leaves the world to darkness and to me.

Now fades the glimmering landscape on the sight,
And all the air a solemn stillness holds,
Save where the beetle wheels his droning flight,
And drowsy tinklings lull the distant folds;

Save that from yonder ivy-mantled tow'r
The mopeing owl does to the moon complain
Of such, as wand'ring near her secret bow'r,
Molest her ancient solitary reign.

Beneath those rugged elms, that yew-tree's shade,
Where heaves the turf in many a mould'ring heap,
Each in his narrow cell for ever laid,
The rude Forefathers of the hamlet sleep.

The breezy call of incense-breathing Morn,
The swallow twitt'ring from the straw-built shed,
The cock's shrill clarion, or the ecchoing horn,
No more shall rouse them from their lowly bed.

For them no more the blazing hearth shall burn,
Or busy housewife ply her evening care:
No children run to lisp their sire's return,
Or climb his knees the envied kiss to share.

Oft did the harvest to their sickle yield,
Their furrow oft the stubborn glebe has broke;
How jocund did they drive their team afield!
How bow'd the woods beneath their sturdy stroke!

Let not Ambition mock their useful toil,
Their homely joys, and destiny obscure;
Nor Grandeur hear with a disdainful smile,
The short and simple annals of the poor.

The boast of heraldry, the pomp of pow'r,
And all that beauty, all that wealth e'er gave,
Awaits alike th' inevitable hour.
The paths of glory lead but to the grave.

Break, Break, Break

ALFRED, LORD TENNYSON

Break, break, break,
   On thy cold grey stones, O Sea!
And I would that my tongue could utter
   The thoughts that arise in me.

O well for the fisherman's boy,
   That he shouts with his sister at play!
O well for the sailor lad,
   That he sings in his boat on the bay!

And the stately ships go on
   To their haven under the hill;
But O for the touch of a vanish'd hand,
   And the sound of a voice that is still!

Break, break, break
   At the foot of thy crags, O Sea!
But the tender grace of a day that is dead
   Will never come back to me.

Lights Out

EDWARD THOMAS

I have come to the borders of sleep,
The unfathomable deep
Forest where all must lose
Their way, however straight,
Or winding, soon or late;
They cannot choose.

Many a road and track
That, since the dawn's first crack,
Up to the forest brink,
Deceived the travellers,
Suddenly now blurs,
And in they sink.

Here love ends,
Despair, ambition ends;
All pleasure and all trouble,
Although most sweet or bitter,
Here ends in sleep that is sweeter
Than tasks most noble.

There is not any book
Or face of dearest look
That I would not turn from now
To go into the unknown
I must enter, and leave, alone.
I know not how.

The tall forest towers;
Its cloudy foliage lowers
Ahead, shelf above shelf;
Its silence I hear and obey
That I may lose my way
And myself.

Annabel Lee

EDGAR ALLAN POE

It was many and many a year ago,
    In a kingdom by the sea,
That a maiden there lived whom you may know
    By the name of ANNABEL LEE;
And this maiden she lived with no other thought
    Than to love and be loved by me.

I was a child and *she* was a child,
    In this kingdom by the sea,
But we loved with a love that was more than love –
    I and my ANNABEL LEE;
With a love that the wingèd seraphs of Heaven
    Coveted her and me.

And this was the reason that, long ago,
    In this kingdom by the sea,
A wind blew out of a cloud, chilling
    My beautiful ANNABEL LEE;
So that her highborn kinsman came
    And bore her away from me,
To shut her up in a sepulchre
    In this kingdom by the sea.

The angels, not half so happy in Heaven,
    Went envying her and me –
Yes! – that was the reason (as all men know,
    In this kingdom by the sea)
That the wind came out of the cloud by night,
    Chilling and killing my ANNABEL LEE.

But our love it was stronger by far than the love
    Of those who were older than we –
    Of many far wiser than we –
And neither the angels in Heaven above,
    Nor the demons down under the sea,
Can ever dissever my soul from the soul
    Of the beautiful ANNABEL LEE.

For the moon never beams, without bringing me dreams
    Of the beautiful ANNABEL LEE;
And the stars never rise, but I feel the bright eyes
    Of the beautiful ANNABEL LEE;
And so, all the night-tide, I lie down by the side
    Of my darling – my darling – my life and my bride,
    In her sepulchre there by the sea,
    In her tomb by the sounding sea.

ALL SORTS OF FUNNY THOUGHTS: POEMS REMEMBERED FROM CHILDHOOD

Poetry is always among the first scraps of language that we absorb as very young children. Nursery rhymes, nonsense limericks and verse stories from our earliest days stay with us throughout the years, and I hope this selection ignites pleasurable nostalgia for the dread inspired by Belloc's *Cautionary Tales* or the magic of a childhood Christmas. There is always time to visit old friends, from Christopher Robin to Mr Toad, and look again for a moment through a child's eyes – especially if you have the opportunity to introduce new young readers to these colourful worlds.

Daddy Fell Into the Pond

ALFRED NOYES

Everyone grumbled. The sky was grey.
We had nothing to do and nothing to say.
We were nearing the end of a dismal day,
And there seemed to be nothing beyond,
    THEN
    Daddy fell into the pond!

And everyone's face grew merry and bright,
And Timothy danced for sheer delight.
'Give me the camera, quick, oh quick!
He's crawling out of the duckweed.' *Click!*

Then the gardener suddenly slapped his knee,
And doubled up, shaking silently,
And the ducks all quacked as if they were daft
And it sounded as if the old drake laughed.

Oh, there wasn't a thing that didn't respond
    WHEN
    Daddy fell into the pond!

Halfway Down

A. A. MILNE

Halfway down the stairs
Is a stair
Where I sit.
There isn't any
Other stair
Quite like
It.
I'm not at the bottom,
I'm not at the top;
So this is the stair
Where
I always
Stop.

Halfway up the stairs
Isn't up
And isn't down.
It isn't in the nursery,
It isn't in the town.
And all sorts of funny thoughts
Run round my head:

'It isn't really
Anywhere!
It's somewhere else
Instead!'

The Lamplighter

ROBERT LOUIS STEVENSON

My tea is nearly ready and the sun has left the sky;
It's time to take the window to see Leerie going by;
For every night at teatime and before you take your seat,
With lantern and with ladder he comes posting up the street.

Now Tom would be a driver and Maria go to sea,
And my papa's a banker and as rich as he can be;
But I, when I am stronger and can choose what I'm to do,
O Leerie, I'll go round at night and light the lamps with you!

For we are very lucky, with a lamp before the door,
And Leerie stops to light it as he lights so many more;
And O! before you hurry by with ladder and with light,
O Leerie, see a little child and nod to him to-night!

A Visit from St Nicholas

CLEMENT C. MOORE

'Twas the night before Christmas, when all through the
    house
Not a creature was stirring, not even a mouse;
The stockings were hung by the chimney with care
In hopes that St. Nicholas soon would be there;
The children were nestled all snug in their beds,
While visions of sugar-plums danced in their heads;
And mamma in her kerchief, and I in my cap,
Had just settled our brains for a long winter's nap,
When out on the lawn there arose such a clatter,
I sprang from the bed to see what was the matter.
Away to the window I flew like a flash,
Tore open the shutters and threw up the sash.
The moon on the breast of the new-fallen snow
Gave the lustre of mid-day to objects below,
When, what to my wondering eyes should appear,
But a miniature sleigh, and eight tiny reindeer,
With a little old driver, so lively and quick,
I knew in a moment it must be St Nick.
More rapid than eagles his coursers they came,
And he whistled, and shouted, and called them by name;
'Now, *Dasher!* now, *Dancer!* now, *Prancer* and *Vixen!*

On, *Comet!* on, *Cupid!* on, *Donner* and *Blitzen!*
To the top of the porch! to the top of the wall!
Now dash away! dash away! dash away all!'
As dry leaves that before the wild hurricane fly,
When they meet with an obstacle, mount to the sky;
So up to the house-top the coursers they flew,
With the sleigh full of Toys, and St Nicholas too.
And then, in a twinkling, I heard on the roof
The prancing and pawing of each little hoof.
As I drew in my head, and was turning around,
Down the chimney St Nicholas came with a bound.
He was dressed all in fur, from his head to his foot,
And his clothes were all tarnished with ashes and soot;
A bundle of Toys he had flung on his back,
And he looked like a pedler just opening his pack.
His eyes – how they twinkled! his dimples how merry!
His cheeks were like roses, his nose like a cherry!
His droll little mouth was drawn up like a bow
And the beard of his chin was as white as the snow;
The stump of a pipe he held tight in his teeth,
And the smoke it encircled his head like a wreath;
He had a broad face and a little round belly,
That shook when he laughed, like a bowlful of jelly.
He was chubby and plump, a right jolly old elf,
And I laughed when I saw him, in spite of myself;
A wink of his eye and a twist of his head,

Soon gave me to know I had nothing to dread;
He spoke not a word, but went straight to his work,
And filled all the stockings; then turned with a jerk,
And laying his finger aside of his nose,
And giving a nod, up the chimney he rose;
He sprang to his sleigh, to his team gave a whistle,
And away they all flew like the down of a thistle.
But I heard him exclaim, ere he drove out of sight,
'Happy Christmas to all, and to all a good-night.'

Matilda: Who told Lies, and was Burned to Death

HILAIRE BELLOC

Matilda told such Dreadful Lies,
It made one Gasp and Stretch one's Eyes;
Her Aunt, who, from her Earliest Youth,
Had kept a Strict Regard for Truth,
Attempted to Believe Matilda:
The effort very nearly killed her,
And would have done so, had not She
Discovered this Infirmity.
For once, towards the Close of Day,
Matilda, growing tired of play,
And finding she was left alone,
Went tiptoe to the Telephone
And summoned the Immediate Aid
Of London's Noble Fire-Brigade.
Within an hour the Gallant Band
Were pouring in on every hand,
From Putney, Hackney Downs, and Bow
With Courage high and Hearts a-glow
They galloped, roaring through the Town,
'Matilda's House is Burning Down!'

Inspired by British Cheers and Loud
Proceeding from the Frenzied Crowd,
They ran their ladders through a score
Of windows on the Ball Room Floor;
And took Peculiar Pains to Souse
The Pictures up and down the House,
Until Matilda's Aunt succeeded
In showing them they were not needed
And even then she had to pay
To get the Men to go away!

It happened that a few Weeks later
Her Aunt was off to the Theatre
To see that Interesting Play
The Second Mrs Tanqueray.
She had refused to take her Niece
To hear this Entertaining Piece:
A Deprivation Just and Wise
To Punish her for Telling Lies.
That Night a Fire *did* break out –
You should have heard Matilda Shout!
You should have heard her Scream and Bawl,
And throw the window up and call
To People passing in the Street –
(The rapidly increasing Heat

Encouraging her to obtain
Their confidence) – but all in vain!
For every time She shouted 'Fire!'
They only answered 'Little Liar!'
And therefore when her Aunt returned,
Matilda, and the House, were Burned.

The Owl and the Pussy-cat

EDWARD LEAR

The Owl and the Pussy-cat went to sea
   In a beautiful pea-green boat,
They took some honey, and plenty of money,
   Wrapped up in a five-pound note.
The Owl looked up to the stars above,
   And sang to a small guitar,
'O lovely Pussy! O Pussy, my love,
   What a beautiful Pussy you are,
      You are,
      You are!
   What a beautiful Pussy you are!'

Pussy said to the Owl, 'You elegant fowl!
   How charmingly sweet you sing!
O let us be married! Too long we have tarried:
   But what shall we do for a ring?'
They sailed away, for a year and a day,
   To the land where the Bong-tree grows
And there in a wood a Piggy-wig stood
   With a ring at the end of his nose,
      His nose,
      His nose,
   With a ring at the end of his nose.

'Dear Pig, are you willing to sell for one shilling
    Your ring?' Said the Piggy, 'I will.'
So they took it away, and were married next day
    By the Turkey who lives on the hill.
They dined on mince, and slices of quince,
    Which they ate with a runcible spoon;
And hand in hand, on the edge of the sand,
    They danced by the light of the moon,
        The moon,
        The moon,
They danced by the light of the moon.

The Lobster Quadrille

LEWIS CARROLL

'Will you walk a little faster?' said a whiting to a snail,
'There's a porpoise close behind us, and he's treading on
    my tail.
See how eagerly the lobsters and the turtles all advance!
They are waiting on the shingle – will you come and join
    the dance?
    Will you, won't you, will you, won't you, will you join
        the dance?
    Will you, won't you, will you, won't you, won't you
        join the dance?

'You can really have no notion how delightful it will be
When they take us up and throw us, with the lobsters,
    out to sea!'
But the snail replied "Too far, too far!" and gave a look
    askance –
Said he thanked the whiting kindly, but he would not
    join the dance.
    Would not, could not, would not, could not, would
        not join the dance.
    Would not, could not, would not, could not, could not
        join the dance.

'What matters it how far we go?' his scaly friend replied.
'There is another shore, you know, upon the other side.
The further off from England the nearer is to France –
Then turn not pale, beloved snail, but come and join the
    dance.
    Will you, won't you, will you, won't you, will you join
        the dance?
    Will you, won't you, will you, won't you, won't you
        join the dance?

The Song of Mr Toad

KENNETH GRAHAME

'The world has held great Heroes,
	As history-books have showed;
But never a name to go down to fame
	Compared with that of Toad!

'The clever men at Oxford
	Know all that there is to be knowed.
But they none of them know one half as much
	As intelligent Mr Toad!

'The animals sat in the Ark and cried,
	Their tears in torrents flowed.
Who was it said, "There's land ahead"?
	Encouraging Mr Toad!

'The army all saluted
	As they marched along the road.
Was it the King? Or Kitchener?
	No. It was Mr Toad.

'The Queen and her Ladies-in-waiting
    Sat at the window and sewed.
She cried, "Look! who's that *handsome* man?"
    They answered, "Mr Toad."

'The motor-car went Poop-poop-poop,
    As it raced along the road.
Who was it steered it into a pond?
    Ingenious Mr Toad!'

The Pig

ROALD DAHL

In England once there lived a big
And wonderfully clever pig.
To everybody it was plain
That Piggy had a massive brain.
He worked out sums inside his head,
There was no book he hadn't read,
He knew what made an airplane fly,
He knew how engines worked and why.
He knew all this, but in the end
One question drove him round the bend:
He simply couldn't puzzle out
What LIFE was really all about.
What was the reason for his birth?
Why was he placed upon this earth?
His giant brain went round and round.
Alas, no answer could be found,
Till suddenly one wondrous night,
All in a flash, he saw the light.
He jumped up like a ballet dancer
And yelled, 'By gum, I've got the answer!'
'They want my bacon slice by slice

'To sell at a tremendous price!
'They want my tender juicy chops
'To put in all the butchers' shops!
'They want my pork to make a roast
'And that's the part'll cost the most!
'They want my sausages in strings!
'They even want my chitterlings!
'The butcher's shop! The carving knife!
'That is the reason for my life!'
Such thoughts as these are not designed
To give a pig great peace of mind.
Next morning, in comes Farmer Bland,
A pail of pigswill in his hand,
And Piggy with a mighty roar,
Bashes the farmer to the floor . . .
Now comes the rather grizzly bit
So let's not make too much of it,
Except that you *must* understand
That Piggy *did eat* Farmer Bland,
He ate him up from head to toe,
Chewing the pieces nice and slow.
It took an hour to reach the feet,
Because there was so much to eat,
And when he'd finished, Pig, of course,
Felt absolutely no remorse.

Slowly he scratched his brainy head
And with a little smile, he said,
'I had a fairly powerful hunch
'That he might have me for his lunch.
'And so, because I feared the worst,
'I thought I'd better eat *him* first.'

Buckingham Palace

A. A. MILNE

They're changing guard at Buckingham Palace –
Christopher Robin went down with Alice.
Alice is marrying one of the guard.
'A soldier's life is terrible hard,'

Says Alice.

They're changing guard at Buckingham Palace –
Christopher Robin went down with Alice.
We saw a guard in a sentry-box.
'One of the sergeants looks after their socks,'

Says Alice.

They're changing guard at Buckingham Palace –
Christopher Robin went down with Alice.
We looked for the King, but he never came.
'Well, God take care of him, all the same,'

Says Alice.

They're changing guard at Buckingham Palace –
Christopher Robin went down with Alice.
They've great big parties inside the grounds.
'I wouldn't be King for a hundred pounds,'

Says Alice.

They're changing guard at Buckingham Palace –
Christopher Robin went down with Alice.
A face looked out, but it wasn't the King's.
'He's much too busy a-signing things,'

Says Alice.

They're changing guard at Buckingham Palace –
Christopher Robin went down with Alice.
'Do you think the King knows all about me?'
'Sure to, dear, but it's time for tea,'

Says Alice.

THE FAMILY FACE: POEMS ABOUT FAMILY AND CHILDHOOD

Not all poetry asks readers to explore far-flung realms or sail distant seas. These verses travel only in time to the poet's vanished childhood, or scrutinise what binds us together in the heart of the family home. Deeply personal, sometimes raw and not always positive, these works manage to speak universally: to the children we used to be as well as to newly minted or almost outgrown parents.

You're

SYLVIA PLATH

Clownlike, happiest on your hands,
Feet to the stars, and moon-skulled,
Gilled like a fish. A common-sense
Thumbs-down on the dodo's mode.
Wrapped up in yourself like a spool,
Trawling your dark as owls do.
Mute as a turnip from the Fourth
Of July to All Fools' Day,
O high-riser, my little loaf.

Vague as fog and looked for like mail.
Farther off than Australia.
Bent-backed atlas, our traveled prawn.
Snug as a bud and at home
Like a sprat in a pickle jug.
A creel of eels, all ripples.
Jumpy as a Mexican bean.
Right, like a well-done sum.
A clean slate, with your own face on.

Fern Hill

DYLAN THOMAS

Now as I was young and easy under the apple boughs
About the lilting house and happy as the grass was green,
   The night above the dingle starry,
     Time let me hail and climb
    Golden in the heydays of his eyes,
And honoured among wagons I was prince of the apple
   towns
And once below a time I lordly had the trees and leaves
     Trail with daisies and barley
    Down the rivers of the windfall light.

And as I was green and carefree, famous among the barns
About the happy yard and singing as the farm was home,
   In the sun that is young once only,
     Time let me play and be
    Golden in the mercy of his means,
And green and golden I was huntsman and herdsman,
   the calves
Sang to my horn, the foxes on the hills barked clear and
   cold,
     And the sabbath rang slowly
    In the pebbles of the holy streams.

All the sun long it was running, it was lovely, the hay
Fields high as the house, the tunes from the chimneys, it
was air
And playing, lovely and watery
And fire green as grass.
And nightly under the simple stars
As I rode to sleep the owls were bearing the farm away,
All the moon long I heard, blessed among stables, the
nightjars
Flying with the ricks, and the horses
Flashing into the dark.

And then to awake, and the farm, like a wanderer white
With the dew, come back, the cock on his shoulder: it was all
Shining, it was Adam and maiden,
The sky gathered again
And the sun grew round that very day.
So it must have been after the birth of the simple light
In the first, spinning place, the spellbound horses walking
warm
Out of the whinnying green stable
On to the fields of praise.

And honoured among foxes and pheasants by the gay house
Under the new made clouds and happy as the heart was
  long,
   In the sun born over and over,
     I ran my heedless ways,
   My wishes raced through the house high hay
And nothing I cared, at my sky blue trades, that time allows
In all his tuneful turning so few and such morning songs
   Before the children green and golden
     Follow him out of grace,

Nothing I cared, in the lamb white days, that time would
  take me
Up to the swallow thronged loft by the shadow of my hand,
   In the moon that is always rising,
     Nor that riding to sleep
   I should hear him fly with the high fields
And wake to the farm forever fled from the childless land.
Oh as I was young and easy in the mercy of his means,
     Time held me green and dying
   Though I sang in my chains like the sea.

Heredity

THOMAS HARDY

I am the family face;
Flesh perishes, I live on,
Projecting trait and trace
Through time to times anon,
And leaping from place to place
Over oblivion.

The years-heired feature that can
In curve and voice and eye
Despise the human span
Of durance – that is I;
The eternal thing in man,
That heeds no call to die.

Piano

D. H. LAWRENCE

Softly, in the dusk, a woman is singing to me;
Taking me back down the vista of years, till I see
A child sitting under the piano, in the boom of the tingling
    strings
And pressing the small, poised feet of a mother who smiles
    as she sings.

In spite of myself, the insidious mastery of song
Betrays me back, till the heart of me weeps to belong
To the old Sunday evenings at home, with winter outside
And hymns in the cosy parlour, the tinkling piano our
    guide.

So now it is vain for the singer to burst into clamour
With the great black piano appassionato. The glamour
Of childish days is upon me, my manhood is cast
Down in the flood of remembrance, I weep like a child for
    the past.

This Be the Verse

PHILIP LARKIN

They fuck you up, your mum and dad.
    They may not mean to, but they do.
They fill you with the faults they had
    And add some extra, just for you.

But they were fucked up in their turn
    By fools in old-style hats and coats,
Who half the time were soppy-stern
    And half at one another's throats.

Man hands on misery to man.
    It deepens like a coastal shelf.
Get out as early as you can,
    And don't have any kids yourself.

Outgrown

PENELOPE SHUTTLE

It is both sad and a relief to fold so carefully
her outgrown clothes and line up the little worn shoes
of childhood, so prudent, scuffed and particular.
It is both happy and horrible to send them galloping
back tappity-tap along the misty chill path into the past.

It is both a freedom and a prison, to be outgrown
by her as she towers over me as thin as a sequin
in her doc martens and her pretty skirt,
because just as I work out how to be a mother
she stops being a child.

THINGS I AM WISER TO KNOW:
WAYS TO LIVE

This final section gathers together poems that provide sage advice, whether you lack courage, contentment or quite enough champagne. From pastoral peace to growing old disgracefully, the poets here present diverse paths to tread, and varied goals to strive for. It seems fitting to close with two poems about the power and value of poetry itself, both as an intimate conversation between poet and reader, and a herald and barometer of the times. These final words of wisdom remind us of the benefits we can reap from our favourite verses, and exactly why we love to read and remember them.

Invictus

WILLIAM ERNEST HENLEY

Out of the night that covers me,
    Black as the Pit from pole to pole,
I thank whatever gods may be
    For my unconquerable soul.

In the fell clutch of circumstance
    I have not winced nor cried aloud.
Under the bludgeonings of chance
    My head is bloody, but unbowed.

Beyond this place of wrath and tears
    Looms but the Horror of the shade,
And yet the menace of the years
    Finds, and shall find, me unafraid.

It matters not how strait the gate,
    How charged with punishments the scroll,
I am the master of my fate:
    I am the captain of my soul.

Still I Rise

MAYA ANGELOU

You may write me down in history
With your bitter, twisted lies,
You may trod me in the very dirt
But still, like dust, I'll rise.

Does my sassiness upset you?
Why are you beset with gloom?
'Cause I walk like I've got oil wells
Pumping in my living room.

Just like moons and like suns,
With the certainty of tides,
Just like hopes springing high,
Still I'll rise.

Did you want to see me broken?
Bowed head and lowered eyes?
Shoulders falling down like teardrops,
Weakened by my soulful cries.

Does my haughtiness offend you?
Don't you take it awful hard
'Cause I laugh like I've got gold mines
Diggin' in my own backyard.

You may shoot me with your words,
You may cut me with your eyes,
You may kill me with your hatefulness,
But still, like air, I'll rise.

Does my sexiness upset you?
Does it come as a surprise
That I dance like I've got diamonds
At the meeting of my thighs?

Out of the huts of history's shame
I rise
Up from a past that's rooted in pain
I rise
I'm a black ocean, leaping and wide,
Welling and swelling I bear in the tide.

Leaving behind nights of terror and fear
I rise
Into a daybreak that's wondrously clear
I rise
Bringing the gifts that my ancestors gave,
I am the dream and the hope of the slave.
I rise
I rise
I rise.

Hope is the Thing with Feathers

EMILY DICKINSON

Hope is the thing with feathers
That perches in the soul,
And sings the tune without the words,
And never stops at all,

And sweetest in the gale is heard;
And sore must be the storm
That could abash the little bird
That kept so many warm.

I've heard it in the chillest land,
And on the strangest sea;
Yet, never, in extremity,
It asked a crumb of me.

When I Was One-and-Twenty

A. E. HOUSMAN

When I was one-and-twenty
  I heard a wise man say,
'Give crowns and pounds and guineas
  But not your heart away;
Give pearls away and rubies
  But keep your fancy free.'
But I was one-and-twenty,
  No use to talk to me.

When I was one-and-twenty
  I heard him say again,
'The heart out of the bosom
  Was never given in vain;
'Tis paid with sighs a plenty
  And sold for endless rue.'
And I am two-and-twenty,
  And oh, 'tis true, 'tis true.

If—

RUDYARD KIPLING

If you can keep your head when all about you
Are losing theirs and blaming it on you;
If you can trust yourself when all men doubt you,
But make allowance for their doubting too;
If you can wait and not be tired by waiting,
Or, being lied about, don't deal in lies,
Or being hated, don't give way to hating,
And yet don't look too good, nor talk too wise;

If you can dream – and not make dreams your master;
If you can think – and not make thoughts your aim;
If you can meet with Triumph and Disaster
And treat those two impostors just the same;
If you can bear to hear the truth you've spoken
Twisted by knaves to make a trap for fools,
Or watch the things you gave your life to, broken,
And stoop and build 'em up with worn-out tools:

If you can make one heap of all your winnings
And risk it on one turn of pitch-and-toss,
And lose, and start again at your beginnings
And never breathe a word about your loss;
If you can force your heart and nerve and sinew
To serve your turn long after they are gone,
And so hold on when there is nothing in you
Except the Will which says to them: 'Hold on!'

If you can talk with crowds and keep your virtue,
Or walk with Kings – nor lose the common touch,
If neither foes nor loving friends can hurt you,
If all men count with you, but none too much;
If you can fill the unforgiving minute
With sixty seconds' worth of distance run,
Yours is the Earth and everything that's in it,
And – which is more – you'll be a Man, my son!

Ode on Solitude

ALEXANDER POPE

Happy the man whose wish and care
    A few paternal acres bound,
Content to breathe his native air
      In his own ground.

Whose herds with milk, whose fields with bread,
    Whose flocks supply him with attire,
Whose trees in summer yield him shade,
      In winter fire.

Bless'd, who can unconcern'dly find
    Hours, days, and years, slide soft away,
In health of body, peace of mind,
      Quiet by day;

Sound sleep by night: study and ease
    Together mix'd; sweet recreation;
And innocence, which most does please,
      With meditation.

Thus let me live, unseen, unknown,
    Thus unlamented let me die;
Steal from the world, and not a stone
      Tell where I lie.

Warning

JENNY JOSEPH

When I am an old woman I shall wear purple
With a red hat which doesn't go, and doesn't suit me.
And I shall spend my pension on brandy and summer gloves
And satin sandals, and say we've no money for butter.
I shall sit down on the pavement when I'm tired
And gobble up samples in shops and press alarm bells
And run my stick along the public railings
And make up for the sobriety of my youth.
I shall go out in my slippers in the rain
And pick the flowers in other people's gardens
And learn to spit.

You can wear terrible shirts and grow more fat
And eat three pounds of sausages at a go
Or only bread and pickle for a week
And hoard pens and pencils and beermats and things in
    boxes.

But now we must have clothes that keep us dry
And pay our rent and not swear in the street
And set a good example for the children.
We must have friends to dinner and read the papers.

But maybe I ought to practise a little now?
So people who know me are not too shocked and surprised
When suddenly I am old, and start to wear purple.

Inventory

DOROTHY PARKER

Four be the things I am wiser to know:
Idleness, sorrow, a friend, and a foe.

Four be the things I'd been better without:
Love, curiosity, freckles, and doubt.

Three be the things I shall never attain:
Envy, content, and sufficient champagne.

Three be the things I shall have till I die:
Laughter and hope and a sock in the eye.

When You Are Old

WILLIAM BUTLER YEATS

When you are old and grey and full of sleep,
And nodding by the fire, take down this book,
And slowly read, and dream of the soft look
Your eyes had once, and of their shadows deep;

How many loved your moments of glad grace,
And loved your beauty with love false or true,
But one man loved the pilgrim soul in you,
And loved the sorrows of your changing face;

And bending down beside the glowing bars,
Murmur, a little sadly, how Love fled
And paced upon the mountains overhead
And hid his face amid a crowd of stars.

[after Ronsard]

Dis Poetry

BENJAMIN ZEPHANIAH

Dis poetry is like a riddim dat drops
De tongue fires a riddim dat shoots like shots
Dis poetry is designed fe rantin
Dance hall style, big mouth chanting,
Dis poetry nar put yu to sleep
Preaching follow me
Like yu is blind sheep,
Dis poetry is not Party Political
Not designed fe dose who are critical.
Dis poetry is wid me when I gu to me bed
It gets into me dreadlocks
It lingers around me head
Dis poetry goes wid me as I pedal me bike
I've tried Shakespeare, respect due dere
But did is de stuff I like.

Dis poetry is not afraid of going ina book
Still dis poetry need ears fe hear an eyes fe hav a look
Dis poetry is Verbal Riddim, no big words involved
An if I hav a problem de riddim gets it solved,
I've tried to be more romantic, it docs nu good for me

So I tek a Reggae Riddim an build me poetry,
I could try be more personal
But you've heard it all before,
Pages of written words not needed
Brain has many words in store,
Yu could call dis poetry Dub Ranting
De tongue plays a beat
De body starts skanking,
Dis poetry is quick an childish
Dis poetry is fe de wise an foolish,
Anybody can do it fe free,
Dis poetry is fe yu an me,
Don't stretch yu imagination
Dis poetry is fe de good of de Nation,
Chant,
In de morning
I chant
In de night
I chant
In de darkness
An under de spotlight,
I pass thru University
I pass thru Sociology
An den I got a dread degree
In Dreadfull Ghettology.

Dis poetry stays wid me when I run or walk
An when I am talking to meself in poetry I talk,
Dis poetry is wid me,
Below me an above,
Dis poetry's from inside me
It goes to yu
   WID LUV.

Ode
[extract]
ARTHUR O'SHAUGHNESSY

We are the music-makers,
   And we are the dreamers of dreams,
Wandering by lone sea-breakers,
   And sitting by desolate streams;
World-losers and world-forsakers,
   On whom the pale moon gleams:
Yet we are the movers and shakers
   Of the world for ever, it seems.

With wonderful deathless ditties
We build up the world's great cities,
   And out of a fabulous story
   We fashion an empire's glory:
One man with a dream, at pleasure,
   Shall go forth and conquer a crown;
And three with a new song's measure
   Can trample an empire down.

We, in the ages lying
   In the buried past of the earth,
Built Nineveh with our sighing,
   And Babel itself in our mirth;
And o'erthrew them with prophesying
   To the old of the new world's worth;
For each age is a dream that is dying,
   Or one that is coming to birth.

Select Bibliography

Abrams, M. H. (ed.), *The Norton Anthology of English Literature, Volume I* (W. W. Norton, 1993)

Abrams, M. H., et al (eds), *The Norton Anthology of English Literature, Volume II* (W. W. Norton, 1993)

Alma, Deborah (ed.), *The Emergency Poet: An Anti-Stress Poetry Anthology* (Michael O'Mara, 2015)

Alma, Deborah (ed.), *The Everyday Poet: Poems to Live By* (Michael O'Mara, 2016)

Barber, Laura (ed.), *Penguin's Poems by Heart: Poetry to Remember and Love For Ever* (Penguin, 2009)

Dove, Rita (ed.), *The Penguin Anthology of Twentieth-Century American Poetry* (Penguin, 2011)

Ferguson, Margaret, Salter, Mary Jo and Stallworthy, Jon (eds), *The Norton Anthology of Poetry* (W. W. Norton, 2005)

Gurr, Elizabeth and de Piro, Celia (eds), *Nineteenth and Twentieth Century Women Poets* (Oxford University Press, 2006)

Hamilton, Ian (ed.), *The Oxford Companion to Twentieth-Century Poetry in English* (Oxford University Press, 1994)

Heaney, Seamus (ed.), *William Wordsworth* (Faber, 2001)

Holmes, Richard, *Blake's Songs of Innocence and Experience* (Tate Publishing, 1991)

Hughes, Ted (ed.), *By Heart: 101 Poems to Remember* (Faber, 1997)

Lonsdale, Roger (ed.), *The New Oxford Book of Eighteenth Century Verse* (Oxford University Press, 1984)

McDonald, Trevor, *Favourite Poems* (Michael O'Mara, 1997)

Milligan, Spike (foreword), *The Nation's Favourite Children's Poems* (BBC, 2001)

Ricks, Christopher (ed.), *The Oxford Book of English Verse* (Oxford University Press, 1999)

Roe, Dinah (ed.), *The Pre-Raphaelites: From Rossetti to Ruskin* (Penguin, 2010)

Sampson, Ana (ed.), *I Wandered Lonely as a Cloud ... And Other Poems You Half-remember from School* (Michael O'Mara, 2009)

Sampson, Ana (ed.), *Poems to Learn by Heart* (Michael O'Mara, 2013)

Sampson, Ana (ed.), *Tyger Tyger, Burning Bright: Much-Loved Poems You Half-remember* (Michael O'Mara, 2011)

Williams, Hugo (ed.), *John Betjeman* (Faber, 2006)

Wordsworth, Jonathan (ed.), *The New Penguin Book of Romantic Poetry* (Penguin, 2005)

Acknowledgements

The author and publishers are grateful to the following for permission to use material that is in copyright:

Maya Angelou: 'Still I Rise', from *And Still I Rise*, published by Little, Brown Book Group.

Matthew Arnold: 'Dover Beach', reproduced by kind permission of Frederick W. Whitridge.

W. H. Auden: 'Funeral Blues' © 1936, 1938 by W. H. Auden. Reprinted by permission of Curtis Brown, Ltd.

Pam Ayres: 'Yes I'll Marry You My Dear', from *With These Hands*, published by Wiedenfeld & Nicolson © Pam Ayres, 1997, 2008. Reproduced by permission of Sheil Land Associates Ltd.

Hilaire Belloc: 'The Elephant' and 'Matilda…', from *Complete Verse*, reprinted by permission of Peters Fraser & Dunlop (www.petersfraserdunlop.com) on behalf of the Estate of Hilaire Belloc.

Wendell Berry: 'The Peace of Wild Things' © 2012 by Wendell Berry, from *New Collected Poems*. Reprinted by permission of Counterpoint.

permission of the author c/o Rogers, Coleridge & White Ltd., 20 Powis Mews, London W11 1JN.

T. S. Eliot: 'The Naming of Cats', from *Old Possum's Book of Practical Cats* by T. S. Eliot, reproduced by permission of the publishers Faber and Faber Ltd.

Robert Frost: 'Stopping by Woods on a Snowy Evening', from *The Poetry of Robert Frost*, ed. Edward Connery Lathem, published by Jonathan Cape. Reprinted by permission of the Random House Group Ltd.

Thom Gunn: 'Considering the Snail', from *Collected Poems*, reproduced by permission of the publishers Faber and Faber Ltd.

F. W. Harvey: 'Ducks', reprinted by kind permission of his daughter, Eileen Ann Griffiths.

Seamus Heaney: 'Blackberry-Picking', from *Death of a Naturalist*, reproduced by permission of the publishers Faber and Faber Ltd.

Jenny Joseph: 'Warning' © Jenny Joseph, *Selected Poems*, Bloodaxe, 1992. Reproduced with permission of Johnson & Alcock Ltd.

Philip Larkin: 'This Be the Verse', from *The Complete Poems*, reproduced by permission of the publishers Faber and Faber Ltd.

Carl Sandburg: 'Fog', from *The Complete Poems of Carl Sandburg* © 1969, 1970 by Lillian Steichen Sandburg. Reprinted by permission of Houghton Mifflin Harcourt Publishing Company. All rights reserved.

Siegfried Sassoon: 'Dreamers' © Siegfried Sassoon, reprinted by kind permission of the Estate of George Sassoon.

Penelope Shuttle: 'Outgrown', from *Selected Poems*, Oxford Poets/Carcanet © Penelope Shuttle, 1998.

Dylan Thomas: 'Fern Hill' and 'Do Not Go Gentle into That Good Night' © The Trustees for the Copyrights of Dylan Thomas, published in *The Collected Poems of Dylan Thomas* (Weidenfeld & Nicolson).

J. R. R. Tolkien: 'Far Over the Misty Mountains Cold', from *The Hobbit*, reprinted by permission of HarperCollins Publishers Ltd © 1937 J. R. R. Tolkien.

Derek Walcott: 'Love After Love', from *The Poetry of Derek Walcott, 1948–2013*, reproduced by permission of the publishers Faber and Faber Ltd.

Benjamin Zephaniah: 'Dis Poetry', from Benjamin Zephaniah's *City Psalms* (Bloodaxe Books, 1992), www.bloodaxebooks.com.

Index of poets

Index of titles, first lines and notable lines

bold type = titles; plain type = first lines; italic type = notable lines; the articles 'the' and 'a(n)' are ignored for sorting purposes.